D1707375

Runners

& Other Dreamers

John L. Parker, Jr.

Cedarwinds Publishing Company

The last eight chapters of this book were released in an earlier version titled *Runners & Others Ghosts on the Trail.*

As with the first version, these pieces are all—to the extent any writer may make the claim—true.

They have appeared in somewhat different form—occasionally, when handled by a particularly disturbed editor, in *much* different form—in *The Runner, Runner's World, Running, Running Times, Ultrasport, Miami Magazine* and *Footnotes.*

The reader of this edition, for better or worse, will have to suffer through my original, unfiltered prose.

J.P.

Published by Cedarwinds Publishing Company
P.O. Box 13618
Tallahassee, Florida 32317
904/224-9261
904/561-0747 (fax)

Orders:
P.O. Box 351
Medway, Ohio 45341
800/548-2388

Front cover photograph by Jeff Johnson
Back cover photograph by Rock Nelson
Manufactured in the United States

Library of Congress Cataloging in Publication Data

Parker, Jr., John L., 1947- Runners and other dreamers.
1. Runners (Sports)—Biography—Addresses, essays, lectures.
2. Running races—Addresses, essays, lectures. I. Title
796.4'26

ISBN 0-915297-24-8

V 10 9 8 7 6 5 4 3 2

Introduction

People who think a race is nothing more than a contest of speed or endurance are missing the larger context. They are missing the zoo.

A race that brings together serious competitors, talented athletes who have devoted their lives to the pursuit of barely comprehensible skills, can be thought of as an exhibition of exotic creatures. These are people who are living their lives differently than most of us, and there is much more of a story to their contest than the simple winning or losing thereof. That, at least, has always been my perspective as a writer on the subject.

Take the runner on the left on the cover of this book, for instance. Shown here barely winning the national USTFF 3-mile title in 1970, his name is Sid Sink, and he was a well-known track runner, and was the most accomplished athlete on a fabled Bowling Green University distance-running juggernaut that included a less-well known runner by the name of Dave Wottle.

Sink looked like a shoe-in for the U.S. Olympic team in 1972 in either the steeplechase or the 5000-meters, but then was hit with the old injury bugaboo (if you look closely, you can see a wrap showing below his shorts on his left leg). It turned out that it was his friend and teammate Wottle (40 yards behind him in the race pictured) who not only made the team, but battled through his own serious injury problems to end up winning the 800-meter gold medal with a thrilling drive in the final straight. (Dave was the one who wore the baseball cap when he ran—as did Sid, you'll notice).

So when I see this picture of Sid leaning into the tape for the win in this picture, it calls up a lot more than a long-forgotten, closely contested footrace.

And, oh yes, the other fellow in the picture is me.

Tallahassee
September, 1988

Also by John L. Parker, Jr.

Once a Runner
The Frank Shorter Story
Guide for the Elite Runner (with Marty Liquori)
Runners & Other Ghosts on the Trail
Aerobic Chic & Other Delusions
Run Down, Fired Up, and Teed Off
And Then the Vulture Eats You (Ed.)
Heart Rate Training for the Compleat Idiot

This book, like its predecessor, *Runners & Other Ghosts on the Trail*, is fondly dedicated to the men of the University of Florida track teams, and the men of the Florida Track Club teams, 1968-1972. You know who you are, you rascals.

Contents

Jim Ryun: A Love Story

Ncc one of us escapes high school unscathed. Try to imagine that it is the early 60's and you are out for your first season of high school cross country. You are one of those tall, skinny, awkward, peg-legged and horned-rimmed guys who are really, you know, *into* mechanical drawing, and you understand at some very deep, primal level that you are one of the "outs." Your clothes aren't cool and you've been cut from every team you ever went out for. Girls don't know you're alive and your only male friends are other guys like you. You are a nerd before they even invented the word.

And of course the thing you want most in the world is that which you most irretrievably cannot have: You want to be loved. You want girls to smile shyly at you and guys to beam with admiration as you walk down those corridors of clanging lockers. Sure, most people have a strong desire to be accepted, to be "popular," but in you it burns with a blue flame. And so in your desperation you turn out for that most egalitarian of all sports, long distance running: Each man silly enough to hang around can have as much suffering as the next.

Then a miracle slowly begins to unfold. In the beginning

1

you're dead last in every practice, but in your first race you run the two-mile course in 11:23, fourth on the B-team. No one, not even you, understands how hot that blue flame burns inside you, how it allows you to run yourself to a standstill every afternoon, pushes you out the door in the pre-dawn black of the approaching Kansas winter. A week later, you *win* the B-team race. Two days after that, in a time trial for the A-team, you run 10:36 and move up to the top seven. By the time the state meet rolls around, you lead your team to the state title with a sixth place finish.

In the spring, still only a sophomore, you run the first serious mile race of your life, finishing a hair behind the defending state champion in 4:32.3. A week later you beat him in 4:26.4 and he becomes the first in a long line of former threats, a quaint memory. Your times, astoundingly, drop week after week and you eventually win the state meet in 4:16.2. Later you run 4:07.8 against mature college runners. A year later, a high school junior, you run the first four-minute mile by a schoolboy. Then with a heart-wrenching effort you make the US Tokyo Olympic team. You are 17, an All-American kid from the Midwest who still has his paper route. The news media can hardly believe it: You are a feature story with legs. A year after that, at the end of your senior year in high school, you beat three-time Olympic gold medalist Peter Snell decisively with a time of 3:55.3.

One year later, in the summer of 1966, as a freshman in college (your fourth season of competition) you run one mile faster than any human has ever run it: 3:51.3. It is your second world record and will not be your last.

You have become a living legend, and no one will ever let you cop a plea of mortality again. For the rest of your life you will be both revered and reviled. You will be poked at, analyzed, cussed out and second-guessed by anyone with the price of a postcard. People call you from exotic locations in the middle of the night. People want your signature, your sweatshirt, a lock of your hair. People want to know your diet, your shoe size, your philosophy of life. People want to be your pen pal, your best buddy, your bride-to-be. You have been known to—literally—run and hide from *people.*

Your name is James Ronald Ryun, you are 19 years old, and all you really wanted was to be loved.

The Holidome hotel in Lawrence, Kansas, is something of a monument to the harsh environment of the American prairies. It is built around a large atrium that contains, along with the usual shops and dining areas, a swimming pool, spa, pool table, ping pong table, exercise room, video game room, and perhaps the only indoor miniature golf course in the free world. It is a building that says: We can *live* in here if we really have to.

But Jim Ryun wore shorts and a T-shirt in deference to the unseasonably mild fall day as he strode into the lobby, looking tan, happy, busy, and undeniably *fit.* There is no mistaking him. At 6-3, with those famous white patches of skin discoloration around the knees and elbows, he is all sharp angles and clean lines, as if God designed him on an Etch-a-sketch. There is nothing inefficient, rounded, or soft in the construction.

He was there to meet a visiting writer, the umpteenth hundredth time for this particular drill, but you would never know it from his manner. ("He is the most patient person in the world," his wife Anne would say, rolling her eyes as if still unable to fathom it after all these years.)

"Hi!" he offers his hand and a smile. He wants to know about your trip, if the accommodations are okay, about whether you have noticed the pool table. And like everyone else in Lawrence this particular fall, he wants you to know how lucky you are not to be out putting snow chains on your tires.

"All right, here is the program," he says, "I'm headed over to the track to do a workout with the [University of Kansas] team, but with one detour to drop off Ben Hur at a friend's house. That sound okay?"

The Ryuns' new Jeep Wagoneer is awash with cassettes of *Ben Hur*, a VCR (borrowed for this special family showing), gloves, balls and kid sporting equipment of every imaginable description, coupons for fast food places, and religious pamphlets and sound cassettes ("Loving God I" and "Loving God II" by Chuck Colson, for example). The flotsam of the Jeep provides ample clues as to the Ryun family lifestyle, but even as he chats about his current training, it takes only a few seconds to be see that Jim Ryun is, more than anything else, a deeply, fervently, and unabashedly religious family man.

"The Lord has really blessed me with many months now of injury-free training," is how he describes his recent workouts. Though he had been a faithful church-goer all his life, for the past several years now he and Anne have been born-again Christians. As such their faith is central to everything, but *everything* they do. In fact, Ryun's recent book, written with Mike Phillips, *In Quest of Gold* is as much the story of Jim and Anne coming to grips with their faith as it is the biography of an Olympic runner.

The *Ben Hur* movie had been a special family treat, but Ryun is concerned—mentions several times in fact—that if such a movie were made nowadays, it would undoubtedly be too graphic for family viewing. "Can you imagine what they would do with the leper scene?" he asks. One does not want to imagine.

After dropping off the cassette and player, he drives to the familiar field house built under the football stadium, the same field house where he changed into running togs every afternoon during his undergraduate days. The workout this afternoon will be a light one, five miles of overdistance followed by some weight-lifting. He has already run once this morning, and he needs to rest up for hard intervals the next day. His training is serious, getting 70-80 miles a week even with three interval sessions and a light day on Sunday. He travels a great deal, speaking at clinics and running road races (one of his main sources of income) and his name still draws crowds though his most famous races took place 15-20 years ago. He is a spokesman for the Glaxo pharmaceutical company, makers of asthma and hay fever medicine, and often talks to youngsters—from his own hard-won experiences—about those breathing problems and sports.

Though he says he isn't competitive in races longer than about 8K, he has clocked a 30:37 10K. He wants to run more on the track, but until he is a full fledged master ("In a year and a half! I know because everyone keeps reminding me," he says) the opportunities are limited.

He lopes out of the field house and toward downtown Lawrence, crunching along on the bright fall leaves on the sidewalks, pointing out the sights along the way. Though he is running close to six minute pace, he shuffles along almost awkwardly, as though his body refuses to operate efficiently at such speeds.

"They're doing some restoration of the downtown area," he says, indicating some buildings. A couple of miles later, looping back onto the well-manicured K.U. campus, he points to a tall dormitory building. "That's Olin Templin Hall, where I lived for three and a half years. Until I married Anne."

He studies the building for a moment, before turning and heading back to the field house. It seems he ran by here for a purpose, now accomplished, and may now go about his business. The visitor is surrounded by landmarks of the Ryun saga, and anyone who followed his story knew about Anne Snider, the petite blond cheerleader from rival Kansas State for whom the word "vivacious" was invented. They had met on a blind date during his sophomore year and married two years later.

Ryun knows every inch of this campus, is proud of its traditions and especially its athletic heroes. Basketball legend Wilt Chamberlain played here. World mile record holder Glen Cunningham was a Jayhawk. ". . . and I'm in there," he says absently, of the alumni center's hall of fame.

"A few years ago if I had had to bet on where I would be living right now, Lawrence is one of the last places I would have picked," he laughs. It is a very distinct laugh that he and Anne both use a lot. It is contains elements of resignation and playfulness, and it means: "The Lord works in mysterious ways." They don't even say it anymore. They just use the laugh.

They had been living happily in Santa Barbara, but growing somehow "restless." The family was outgrowing their house and was planning to add on when an obscure deed restriction was pointed out. They needed 167 signatures on a petition to allow the addition, but fell a single signature short: "This was another confirmation that the Lord wanted us to leave," said Jim. "We came back to Lawrence for the Kansas Relays. Ann and I looked at each other and said 'No, Lord, we don't want to, but yes, this is it, isn't it?' " They found their land that same weekend.

Up until the time he became Olin Templin hall's most illustrious freshman in 1965, Jim Ryun's life had gone very much according to the ambitious plan first suggested by his famous Wichita East coach, Robert "Timmie" Timmons. Timmons had preceded Ryun to K.U. by a year as its head track coach so they were happily reunited there. But after Ryun's sophomore year, very little would ever work out exactly as the brilliant coach and his precocious miler planned.

Ryun would go to two Olympics, travel the world, train in the mountains of Arizona, Colorado, and Nevada, live in Eugene, Oregon, and Santa Barbara, California. He would run great, historic races. But very little would ever again go as planned.

On June 23rd, 1967, in Bakersfield, California, Jim Ryun may have been the fastest miler the human race has yet produced, with due respect to Steve Cram, Sebastian Coe, and Steve Ovett. Some experts believe circumstances overwhelmingly indicate that Ryun was clearly capable of going much *faster* than his new world record of 3:51.1, a mark that would nonetheless stand for eight years. One observer who has thought about that race a great deal is arch-rival Marty Liquori, himself twice ranked number one in the world in the mile:

"There were so many things about that mile, if you look at it. Number one, it was a dirt track and the inside lane was pretty torn up by the time the mile was run. That was always a big factor in those days. Number two, he had already run almost that fast before, and we know that when you reach a certain level and stay there a while, then you break through by two or three seconds. Three, the pace of the race was so uneven, with the last lap in 53.6. Add to that the slower shoes in those days, the fact that Ryun didn't race very much in Europe where the really fast times all come now, all those factors seem to indicate that on that day Ryun may have been the fastest miler we've seen yet."

And Ryun himself, who is not given to rash speculation, does not disagree: "We were not even totally rested. We had run a preliminary heat the night before. But when I finished that race I honestly thought that because it was such an easy race that I would probably improve on it, or that someone else would improve on it, reasonably soon. It was the easiest race of my life up until that time and looking back on it now it was still one of the easiest races I ever ran. It wasn't until the halfway point that I realized that I had led the first half. I thought, well, if you led the first half, you might as well lead the second. So I began accelerating, and as I did I was thinking, now wait a minute, am I going to feel this good with 300 yards to go? But with 300 to go I accelerated even more, and I kept thinking, what's happening? Because it was so *simple*. You always dream of races being that way but then when it actually happens you think, gee, this is great. I wish all of them were this way." Even now his voice is filled with wonder at that race.

After running such a magical race, it would have only been natural for Ryun, and nearly everyone else, to expect to win the gold medal in the next Olympic Games in Mexico City in 1968.

But a cruel formula is at work in the four year cycle of Olympic sports. Some great athletes have been unlucky in the timing of their greatness and thus were denied the ultimate prize. Roger Bannister, history's first four-minute miler, was such an athlete. Other great athletes seemed destined to become sports history's tragic figures, jinxed by circumstances. "Star-crossed" is the term the sports writers use, and it is Jim Ryun's unhappy burden to carry that label all of his days.

Despite months of altitude training, despite being at or near the best shape of his life, despite running himself nearly unconscious in the thin air, Ryun's 3:37.8 was second to altitude-born-and-trained Kip Keino's truly brilliant 3:34.9. It is now nearly universally accepted that the Mexico City Olympics were a cruel fraud for sea-level distance runners. Though disappointed, Ryun had understood all along what he was up against. He came back to Lawrence nursing no small satisfaction from the knowledge that he had done his absolute best, that he had run faster than he thought possible at altitude, and that he owned the silver medal.

He could not possibly have been prepared for the absurd criticism of some observers that he had "let his country down."

"I think the turning point was 1968 when he got second running one of the great performances of all time," said Liquori. "When someone insinuates that you let your country down, that may be the worst thing they could say to you. He should have realized he did a great job and the public should have realized it. But they didn't. They felt he was a failure. I think he gave up on himself a little bit after that."

Ryun plowed right back into the collegiate racing grind at K.U. It was a big mistake. He describes it in his book:

"I should have stopped, taken six months off, and then eased back into running gradually, but this was my senior year. I had to compete one more season to fulfill my scholarship obligations. So I continued to run while not enjoying it. I was determined to gut it out even though I was going through the motions mechanically. Running was laborious, school difficult, interviews artificial . . . . I *had* to run . . . I had to win!"

But even Jim Ryun could no longer take winning for granted. The young Marty Liquori had come into his own as a middle distance runner, and he would concede not an inch to Ryun. In the NCAA indoor mile they fought to a dead heat, with the controversial decision going to Ryun. In the outdoor championships in Knoxville, Tennessee, Liquori handed Ryun a decisive loss, 3:57.7 to 3:59.2. Two weeks later, warming up for a preliminary heat of the AAU national championships in Miami, a mentally exhausted Ryun made a weary gesture at the steamy track where the nation's best trackmen were warming up, and asked no one in particular: "How do you get psyched up for *this?*" The next day, a lap and a half into the final, Ryun simply stepped off the track. Ducking everyone, Ryun, Anne and longtime friend Rich Clarkson climbed into a car and disappeared. He wouldn't run again for a full year.

At the time he didn't know if he would ever run again. Munich was three long years away, and even Jim Ryun didn't know how badly he would want to win back the love and acceptance he felt in his heart he had lost.

The Jim Ryun family these days is approximately what you would get if you crossed Donny and Marie Osmond with the Brady Bunch. They live in a beautiful natural wood home they recently built atop a hill in the rolling farmland outside Lawrence. Well, they don't live there so much as percolate in and out of it. Driving up the hill to this house in the late afternoon sun is like ascending into a family sit-com.

Heather, pretty and graceful as a swan at 15, delights her father in finessing rings around the boys in her soccer league. " 'That girl Heather did this, and that girl Heather did that' this fellow was saying at one game," Ryun chuckles. "It was great! He was standing right beside us and didn't know who we were."

Ned and Drew, 12, are identical twins, miniature bookend Jim Ryuns, complete with the horned rim glasses. They are a whirl of motion, athletic as all get-out and brainy: They read voraciously. They carry their baseball gloves and a tennis ball with them everywhere, and pop deadly accurate knucklers and curve balls back and forth every time they get a few minutes. Like most sets of twins, they are self-contained. They finish each other's sentences. They are a constant delight to their mother, who is an easy laugh anyway. After taking on their Dad and a visitor in a game of deck tennis, they want to talk about their favorite book, a civil war novel.

Catharine, 10, clearly taking after her energetic mother, is a budding gymnast. "We have become accustomed," says Ryun "to seeing Catharine transporting herself around the house by just about any method other than walking on two feet." In a burger palace only the evening before she has been persuaded (with very little prodding) to demonstrate the correct form for a cartwheel, which she executes to enthusiastic applause.

At dinner the family holds hands around the table as Ryun offers one of his chatty, personalized prayers, thanking God for the beautiful day, asking for help for friends sick or otherwise in need. The kids have all pitched in to help Anne with a wonderful lasagna, salad, fresh bread and muffins: They are pretty proud of themselves.

As a matter of fact, this is a family that exudes so much energy that it soon becomes clear that papa Ryun, who is not exactly a slouch in that department, seems to be regarded by his brood as something of a lovable frump. They buzz around him, bees to his sunflower.

Later, in the living room, Anne Ryun talks quietly about the years leading up to Munich, her mouth set in a sad smile. She talks of the financial hardships in those "shamateur" pre-running-boom days, about U-Hauling it with kids and furniture from Lawrence to Eugene, and then a year later to California after it was clear the Oregon pollen would make Ryun's comeback training impossible. She talks of the wonderful sense of peace and relief they felt as their newfound faith took hold.

"You just can't imagine the stresses," she says softly, her eyes growing moist with the memories. "If it hadn't been for Jesus Christ I honestly don't know where we would have ended up . . . in an insane asylum . . . in a divorce . . . in . . ." She tries but can think of no worse scenario.

"You know," she said, now weeping openly, "Jim truly no longer cares that he didn't get the gold medal. Did you ask him that? Did you ask him if he wants a gold medal? I know what he would say. But I think Satan . . ."

She pauses and struggles to find her voice among the tears.

"I think Satan really must have had something to do with Jim's falling in that race . . ." In her mind's eye she would be replaying once more that quintessentially tragic scene from modern Olympic sports: history's greatest miler lying briefly unconscious while his dream disappears down the track, never to return.

"They said it was me. They said that he never ran well again after we were married. Only Satan would have kept him from winning that gold medal and showing them that it wasn't me . . ." she says.

Jim was not the only Ryun wounded so terribly by his fall and the maddening callousness of the officials who refused to consider his appeal. But he was the quicker to heal.

And he was quicker to perceive at long last what he considered to be the force at work behind all the years of trials and tribulations since he first stepped out on the cross country field that fall day long ago at Wichita East high school.

"God taught me a very important lesson and that is simply that there is more to life than running. And he also taught me the very deep meaning of forgiveness and forgetting and moving on. I have had the fortune to know people who *are* gold medalists, and many of them aren't all that happy with their lives.

"I'm not trying to justify what took place, but after 12 painful years of the media saying 'Hey, don't give me that God stuff, how can you live without a gold medal?' I can tell you that it's pretty simple. You go on every day and it really isn't such a tragedy. In a sense you have a better perspective on life, because there are a lot more people out there who haven't won a gold medal than who have."

Anne Ryun never stays sad for long. She is back upstairs, laughing with the girls, getting everyone settled for bed. She bounds down the stairs to bid the visitor good-bye, and Jim walks him to the car. Ryun had run 16 quarters in 67 seconds each that afternoon and was feeling pretty good about it. The workout had called for 20 repeats, but he had felt a twinge in one calf and eased off. "That's one difference between now and then," he smiled. "In the old days I would have just gutted it right on through." But the miler has nothing he must prove any more. He can run just for the enjoyment of feeling the wind on his face if he likes, and he likes that very much.

He turns and goes back inside the house on a hill over-looking miles of those rolling Kansas fields, overlooking a place where he made a considerable amount of sports history. He goes back inside a house filled to the rafters with love.

And that, after all, is all Jim Ryun wanted in the first place.

January, 1986

Current edition note: Jim Ryun, plagued by injuries, has had little success as a masters runner. In November of 1996, however, he was elected to Congress, representing his home state of Kansas.

The Teevee Olympics

There I was, recuperating in the hospital from some long-overdue dental surgery on my lower jaw, mouth wired up tighter than John Candy in Spandex, every conceivable nourishment known to civilized man (that would slide through a straw or drip into an IV tube) a mere registered nurse away, a no-nonsense institutional color television set bolted to the wall at an ergonomically determined angle.

Eyes peering out of a mass of bandages, connected to the world by a channel selector, I was what you might call a Rabid TeeVee Spectator of the 23rd Olympiad. I was spaced out, tuned in, and available 24 hours a day. I saw it all, God help me.

Actually, it was not a bad way to see the Olympics, all in all, particularly if you weren't really interested in a trip to the city that writer Benjamin Stein calls "the derationalized zone." But any assessment of such a mammoth undertaking as the televising of the LA Olympics is going to be a good news/bad news type of deal any way you slice it, so if I nick a sacred cow or two's along the way, hey, I'm sorry, it's the kind of guy I am, okay?

First I've got to admit to some prejudices and partialities. I do not think people in red waiters' jackets riding horsies over rows of bushes is the Olympics. I do not think little girls dancing around with beach balls or little strips of crepe paper is the Olympics. And I most especially don't think two ladies in waterproof make-up doing underwater splits to "Bolero" is the Olympics (no matter how many grueling luncheons Esther Williams bravely endured with the string-pullers of the L.A.O.C. to make it happen).

After all, the Olympics started 2760 years ago on a plain in the western Peloponnesus as a track meet. These days, Lord knows, the poor track and field athletes get precious little attention in the American sporting scene as it is, but once every four years the Olympics have given them a chance to take center stage once again.

Over the past several decades, however, we've undergone a kind of event-inflation in the Games. Now it's become *runaway* inflation. After 30 seconds of team handball (or *field hockey,* for crying out loud) I'm ready to get down on all fours and chew big hunks out of the wainscoting.

Often the so-called "expert" commentating on sporting events has approximately the same effect on me. For instance, Howard Cosell may know the shoe size number of every cornerback who ever played Pop Warner football, but any athlete can tell the guy couldn't catch a Frisbee with both hands. Many of his comments clearly reveal that he's never played any kind of sport at all (unless you count bobbing for apples or sack races).

Erich Segal's television commentating on the Munich and Montreal marathons fell in the same category. Who can ever forget his astonishing little feature on the marathoners' "typical" pre-race meal (". . . yes, Jim, and then after the mashed potatoes, the pancakes, the spaghetti and the plate of brownies, most of us marathoners will have a gallon of ice cream or so . . .") or his chauvinistic wrong-headedness in '76 when we were repeatedly told Cierpinski was just about to fall on his face.

This time around ABC made giant strides forward in the

area of commentating, and here I have to admit some partiality.

Marty Liquori is my friend and has been for a long time. We think a lot alike about running and we even wrote a book about training together. Nonetheless, I don't think I'm unduly prejudiced when I say that Marty's commentating on the running events was simply excellent in every respect. He was well-prepared, insightful, and managed to be thoroughly professional without seeming to be an automaton like so many of the beautiful talking heads we are accustomed to seeing on our screens.

Likewise, O.J. Simpson did a good job on the men's sprints (though without Marty's truly keen analytical ability), but Wilma Rudolph, not very well prepared and somewhat ill-at-ease, had her problems. In the 200 final, for instance, she kept talking about the need to "attack the first 200."

There isn't a whole lot involved in sprint coverage, and since TV people think in terms of 10- and 20-second time periods anyway, it's a natural for them. There was a tendency to "Lewis" us to death (more on that later), but that was to be expected. Here's a question for ABC, though: Valerie Brisco-Hooks won only one less gold medal than Carl, and ABC didn't generate nearly the hoopla over her. We don't even know if she has a phone in her car. Maybe somebody ought to teach her how to long jump or pole vault.

The network was particularly good about covering those incredible battles in the men's 800 and 1500. Even the heats and semis were historical races all by themselves. The images are indelibly etched in my mind: Ovett's gut-wrenching dive to qualify in 4th place in his semi (and how much it cost him as he faded badly in the finals); Joaquim Cruz's magisterial power and control in every race, winning the 800 final going away in the third fastest time ever; Coe's tremendous victory in the 1500 and his heartfelt gesture to the British press (in the manner of a true champion, negating a billion silly words with a single heroic deed).

The women were given somewhat short shrift. Not much was made of Kim Gallagher's silver medal in the 800, nor Judi Brown's silver in the 400 hurdles. And I would like to have heard more about Ruth Wysocki (who finished 6th in the 800 and 8th in the 1500). Did the heats and semis get to her? Did she have a cold? The network should have paid more attention to the runner who out-muscled Decker in the 1500 trials.

My own prejudices may be showing through again, but the women's marathon was a joy to behold, with Joanie putting it all into perspective for those deluded souls who thought her world record was suspect because she was "paced" by men.

This time it was Billy Rodgers who was with her every step of the way (wasn't he great?), but he was in the camera truck. We can only dream about what Joan Benoit might have wrought had the conditions been ideal. Bob Sevene, her coach, has been telling us all along that she had been doing the kind of training that could allow her to simply destroy the rest of the field. He was right. Nonetheless, Grete Waitz couldn't have been a more gracious silver medalist, and Rosa Mota of Portugal was so obviously thrilled with the bronze that her joy was infectious. The women marathoners did themselves proud, and you sure can't complain about the coverage. There isn't much of a way to blow a one-woman exhibition.

The coverage of the men's marathon was disastrous. Thrilling though Lopes' victory was, this event was a ludicrous parody of a competitive long distance foot-race, rivaled only by the high-altitude farce in Mexico City in 1968.

The men who were the biggest factors in the race were never on the screen at all. I'm talking about those demented souls on the Los Angeles Organizing Committee who conspired with equally demented television geniuses to start that race in the late afternoon sun so as to catch the prime time audience. Those conditions, it became obvious from watching the runners, could only be described as horrible, if not life-threatening. Surely the sad spectacle of Switzerland's Gabriella Andersen-Shiess staggering last lap in the much cooler women's marathon gives us some slight insight into what the men were going through. Nearly all the men were all thoroughly drenched with sweat by the second mile.

I'm not taking anything away from the truly awesome Olympic record performance of Carlos Lopes, or from the surprising and courageous Treacy and Spedding. All of them would have been factors in that race under *any* circumstances. And I'm aware that it wasn't as hot as everyone thought it would be. But in conditions even *approaching* normal, it would have been an entirely different race. Seko, DeCostella, and Salazar and who knows how many others should have been factors but just couldn't hack the conditions. Runners, no matter how well acclimated they become, simply have tremendously different heat tolerances (I became convinced of that while running along many afternoons behind a dry-backed, comfortable Frank Shorter as the rest of us turned to mush in the 90-degree Gainesville heat).

In terms of ABC's coverage, both Marty and Billie did a fine job again, but did you notice anything peculiar while watching the race? That's right: *we missed every important turning point of the entire race.* Once again, a sad commentary on the running sophistication of TV sports folks is the fact that during every crucial juncture in an Olympic marathon we were off diddling around with a commercial, or an Up-Close-and-Personal, or a nice wide-angled shot of the crowd milling around in the stadium waiting for the finish and the fireworks. We missed Seko's dropping off pace, the lead pack breaking away, DeCostella's dropping back, and Lopes' final break from Spedding and Treacy. There's no telling what else.

I understand the necessity for commercials, but couldn't they have gotten many of them out of the way early in the race so that we could actually *see* the racing when it started to happen?

Maybe I should have known better than to have gotten my hopes up. TV people understand car chases. They understand Loni Anderson pole vaulting half-naked over a pit of writhing

jaguars. They *don't* understand the subtleties of distance racing, and that it doesn't have to be boring (if they'd care to
watch a hot 10K in a European meet some time, they'd get the
message).

But they never seem to learn, and perhaps that is why they
simply decreed that the 10,000 meters never happened in this
Olympics.

Or at least if it did, they played the tape so late I had finally gone to bed. You see, I had a copy of what must have been
regarded as a national security document during the Games: an
actual schedule of the track and field events. ABC never gave
us the slightest hint when track events would be on. But I
knew what was happening on the track while we TV viewers
got to watch Togo and Pango Pango get it on in water polo.
(And by the way, did you notice that while Carl Lewis was
winning his historic fourth gold medal in the 4 X 100 relay, we
were watching—live—some springboard diver from Kuwait.
Seriously.)

To this day I do not know how Alberto Cova pulled off his
gold medal in the 10K. The only reason I know he won at all
was that it was there in glorious agate type in my morning
newspaper.

By the time the 5000 rolled around, I was on to ABC's
tricks. Saturday night at 10:30 p.m. EST, when the 5000 was
being run live, we were constrained to watch a couple of
debt-ridden third world nations duke it out in badminton (at
least that's the way I remember it; I was so mad I couldn't sit
still). But I got some coffee, propped myself up, and outwaited
the bastards. Sure enough, around two a.m., *after* (and this is
no joke) they aired a really scintillating team handball battle
between Yugoslavia and West Germany, I saw what Marty
called (and I had to agree) "the greatest 5000-meter race ever
run."

It was fast from gun to tape (never more than a few ticks
off world record pace), Antonio Leitao keeping the pace siz-
zling around world record levels the whole way while the

famous kickers, including American Doug Padilla, fell back one by one. It had it all: great stars, a bold strategy, an incredible pace, and dangerous kickers hanging on for dear life. To cap if off there were the thrilling kicks of Said Aouita and surprising Swiss Marcus Ryffel for the gold and silver, and the gutsy sprint of pace-setter Leitao to salvage the bronze. And there it was for every insomniac/runner who happened to be tuned in. (I've got it all on tape if someone out there by some miracle has the 10K and wants to trade.)

I don't know, maybe I'm mistaken about the degree of spectator interest in TV land but it seems to me that since millions of Americans actually *run* the 5K and 10K distances (albeit on the roads, generally) they have far more than a passing interest in these events. I mean, these days people *know* how incredible a sub 4:20 first mile in a distance race is. Maybe network execs will figure that kind of thing out one of these days. After all, the reason so many people watch golf isn't because it's inherently thrilling. It's because they've all tried to hit that little white ball with a stick themselves. Are you listening, Roone?

There was, of course, a tremendous amount of coverage on the Decker/Budd collision, and it was warranted, although most of the commentary was obtuse, nationalistic, and completely missed the point.

I have to say that had it not been for Marty's concise (and fairly courageous) reversal of his earlier condemnation of Zola Budd, probably 99.9 per cent of the viewing audience would have been misled as to Zola's blame in what was admittedly a truly sad and tragic occurrence. The other ABC commentators obviously didn't have a clue as to whose fault it was, and they were more than willing to buy Mary's point of view without a second thought. I kept hoping we'd get to hear from Zola personally, but it never happened. Maybe Zola wasn't giving interviews, but if ABC tried to get one, no one mentioned it. Ever hear of balanced reporting, guys? (Along the same lines, the criticism that too much coverage was focused on American athletes was probably well-taken. It wasn't so much that it was wrong, but that it lacked grace and courtesy.)

As to whose fault Mary's fall was, her former husband, marathoner Ron Tabb, summed it up better than anyone when he said that neither Zola *or* Mary had much experience running in a pack. That was the most insightful comment I saw about the incident, and it came from the newspaper, not ABC."

When we heard from Zola, again it was via the newspapers, not from television. Her simple statement that she was sorry it happened and that she hoped she and Mary would race again some time, showed grace and maturity far beyond her years, qualities one could only wish the enormously talented Decker would have developed by now.

We ought to constantly remind ourselves that the Olympic Games are games nonetheless, and that some of the greatest runners who ever lived, runners like Roger Bannister and the great Aussie Ron Clarke, never won Olympic medals. Americans, our sporting sensibilities far too influenced by the dramatic conventions of simple-minded screenwriters, make winning too important and excellence not important enough. Those athletes who buy into that ethic are sadder people for it.

And while we're on the darker side of American sport, we might as well finish up with Carl Lewis, an admittedly historic figure in track and field.

First, there was the mildly disturbing—and well-written— piece on him by Gary Smith in the *Sports Illustrated* Olympic preview issue. Then during the games we began getting those puzzling, slightly negative stories about Lewis in the newspapers. Finally he emerged on the screen and frankly, when the guy wasn't actually running or jumping, he demonstrated clearly why we had been reading all those stories.

His egocentricity, arrogance and coldness, his absolute disdain for others, came across as only TV can deliver it. Both the press and the American public are accustomed to cocky athletes, but Carl Lewis is something else again. Here we have not the tongue-in-cheek braggadocio of Ali. Nor the sly, good-humored swagger of Joe Namath. What we have here is the bald, selfish, humorless materialism of a young man who believes he deserves everything he gets because he has talent, does his workouts, and listens to his agent.

It wasn't just that in the long jump he acted like an impatient bus passenger waiting around to get his ticket punched. And it wasn't his obvious lack of empathy for his fellow athletes, both of which came across clearly on TV. No, it was more than that. When Carl spoke into the cameras, it was clear that his image consultants have done quite a job. The term "well-oiled" comes to mind. But it was *what he said* that was the most damning. He was always protesting that he was misunderstood, that the other athletes were jealous of the attention he received, that being a celebrity was *so* draining, that he had so many career options that it was all becoming just *too* much to deal with. Every third word out of his mouth was endorsement.

There is a word for a guy like Carl Lewis, and that word is "insufferable."

Little wonder the other athletes have no use for him. And I don't buy his claim that it's because he gets so much media attention. We've had plenty of "good copy" athletes in the past who were still beloved of fans and teammates alike. The rest of the Yankees didn't secretly sneer at Mickey Mantle.

I kept hoping some little something would go wrong in Lewis's carefully orchestrated, robot-like march to the four golds. Nothing serious, maybe that he'd get a pimple on the end of his nose before an awards ceremony.

In the final analysis, Carl Lewis represents in microcosm a warped view of sports that is becoming more and more prevalent in America and television has had a lot to do with it.) We've become so wrapped up in images and perceptions that the poor swimmer who didn't give "good reaction" after winning his gold medal was practically drummed out of the Games. He apologized profusely to the television audience and promised "a two-for-one-reaction" after his next win. Maybe he was worried about losing a product deal.

What Carl Lewis and some of the others haven't quite figured out yet is that no matter how many movies he makes, products he endorses, or deals he makes, *it really doesn't ever get any better than it is right now.*

It doesn't get any better than being 23 years old, leading out of the turn with the smell of cut grass in the air and the spring sunshine on your shoulders, feeling *the power* in your legs as you pull away from the field and the stands go crazy . . .

But poor Carl just can't seem to wait to move on to the deodorant commercials. It's very sad.

Both Carl Lewis and Mary Decker ought to pay more attention to that wonderful, wonderful grinning Brit, Daley Thompson, who won the decathlon and who obviously had the time of his life doing it.

As Kenny Moore wrote of him: "Thompson . . . knows he has the most envied life. Those other pursuits [politics, finance, war] are all symbols of what he does . . . They are vicarious, perhaps sublimations, never as intensely satisfying as what he does. Most athletes learn this, with a wrench or a gray, slow dawning, only after they can no longer be athletes—when they have to take up their own secondary pursuit."

On the other hand, maybe Kenny is too pessimistic. If we wait around long enough, all those "secondary pursuits" will end up as Olympics events anyway. I'm lobbying for lawn darts in '92.

October, 1984

Rare Atmosphere, Astringent Light

A high desert, like a war, is a very good place to find out some things about yourself that you may not have wanted to know. How you handle it is your business. It has always been a favorite of Saints and Madmen and Lost Tribes. A lot of people just leave. The Light gets to them. Or the Space. Or something quite a bit less ethereal, such as the way rattlesnakes like to crawl into your sleeping bag to stay warm. The letters back, though, are always wistful:

> . . . I was born and raised in Alamosa. I love every inch of the valley and all the happy memories it holds, and yes, even the sad ones . . .

And:

> . . . My grandfather settled in the valley not awfully long after the Indians left! Talk about "soul"—Mine lies deep in that river land surrounded by the Rockies.

Those lines from a literary magazine called "Alma," Spanish for "soul," published out of Alamosa, Colorado, a small

town on the floor of the San Luis Valley. "Floor" here is deceptive usage. Alamosa is 1½ miles above sea level. And anywhere
you go from here is up. To live in such a place is to break yourself of your oxygen habit.

And there is something else about the high desert, something you think you already know, but which if you haven't
been there you can't really *feel*. It is this: the desert doesn't
care what kind of hurry you're in or how fast you're going, it's
not going to let you get anywhere. You can sit in your
rent-a-car going just under a hundred in a perfectly straight
line toward the airport at Denver and after a couple of hours
you will still be, relatively speaking, in the same place.

You cannot breathe here and you cannot make any
progress against the backdrop. It is the long distance runner's
most perfectly articulated nightmare.

Pat Porter, a 26-year-old Olympian, a four-time national
cross country champion, voluntarily lives in Alamosa. He *likes*
it. Are you beginning to get the idea?

There are enough oddities about Pat Porter as a runner to
render him a puzzle worth your time. The key to it all is the
Cinnamon Bun Metaphor.

They serve the cinnamon buns, wonderful, huge, old-fash-
ioned things, with lots of fluffy butter on top, at the Campus
Cafe, a favorite Porter hangout across the street from Adams
State College. On a bright, chilly, but pleasant winter morning,
Porter has ordered one of the concoctions, along with a bowl of
oatmeal, and he is holding forth in his polite, cheerful way
about the galaxy of competitive running and his particular
orbit in it.

"The first thing about me is, I'm not a very talented individual," he says matter of factly. "What you see is strictly the
product of hard work." What you see, more to the point, is a
nice looking, slightly cocky, engaging young man who could
maybe pass for a wise-cracking older brother in a family

sit-com. But what comes across most clearly to those who know him well is that Pat Porter is a *nice guy*, sensitive, with a little of the wide-eyed innocent about him (a trait Alamosa has helped to preserve) yet with that little sharpened edge all champions must have concealed somewhere on their persons.

This talentless athlete has run 27:31 on the roads (on a course that turned out to be 250 feet short), and has won the last four consecutive national cross country championships, a feat equaled only by another talentless hard worker named Frank Shorter. In a *workout* Porter has run an 8:30 two-mile, then repeat miles in 4:15, 4:10, 4:08. This is at 7500 feet of altitude where, not to belabor the point, jackrabbits can occasionally be seen gasping for breath.

Yet Porter dutifully ticks off the evidence of his physiological shortcomings for the umpteenth time: As a high schooler in Evergreen, outside Denver, he was a decidedly middle-of the-packer, with a 4:29 mile and a 9:51 two-mile: "Oh, I tried *everything* else first. I went out for football, wasn't any good at that. Wrestling, basketball. No go. But it seemed that in running I might have had some ability. At least I was skinny. But even after I went out for the team, the last thing I wanted to do was run a distance race. I wanted to run the quarter, the 220."

His moderate success in high school was enough to keep him going, especially, as with so many determined youngsters who end up runners by default, in cross country, an event he came to love: "In track you have to share the limelight. Lot's of people win. In cross country there's only one winner." Which is a pretty confident way of looking at things. Another way is that there are several thousand people who do *not* win.

Porter enrolled at Metropolitan State College in Denver, where that fall his coach had the singular unpleasant duty of informing him that even though he had heroically qualified for the NAIA nationals, he wouldn't be making the trip.

"They took the top seven out of the district and I finished seventh. I was really fired up. Then the coach comes up and says, 'I don't have the heart to tell you this, but you can't go.' I said why not? He said, 'We're not even affiliated with the NAIA. Or the NCAA. Nothing. We don't even exist.' I was crushed. I decided that the next year I would transfer to Adams State, which was the biggest distance powerhouse I had ever heard of back then. They were wiping everybody."

The transition brought on the athletic equivalent of culture shock. After a summer of self-motivated training, Coach Joe Vigil's cross country runners traditionally reported in the fall ready to start serious workouts. New guy Pat Porter, thinking himself some kind of stud transfer, had casually jogged a few times the preceding months. He was promptly served up for lunch. "After that first workout, I knew it was going to be a long year," he said grimly.

But he couldn't have been in a better place. A lot of big name schools with big name coaches will take a bunch of 4:08 high school milers and have them running 4:15 in no time. Coach Joe Vigil, *Doctor* (exercise physiology) Joe Vigil, has another approach. As he puts it, leaning back in his office chair, wrinkling his broad, brown forehead in concentration: "I don't think I've *ever* had a high school miler who'd broken 4:25. We just don't get the state champions down here . . ."

Whatever Pat Porter's other attributes, he knows how to pick gurus. Vigil is a powerful-looking man, whose voice resonates with emotion when he speaks of training or of life—or probably when he orders lunch for that matter. He has coached 8 NAIA championship cross country teams, he has inspired six individual NAIA indoor mile champions, he will be coaching US Olympic distance runners in Seoul, he . . . but more on him later.

Suffice it to say the Pat Porters of the world are grist for Joe Vigil's mill. It was a perfect match. When Vigil said 'Jump,' Porter said 'How high and do you want it in yards or meters?'

Before he graduated from Adams State he had won the NAIA national cross country title twice and had beaten the world 15K record holder and the NCAA cross country champion. He had run 29:13 on a cross country course. At altitude. And lately he's *really* gotten good.

In 1984, he made the LA Olympic team in the 10K behind Paul Cummings and Craig Virgin, after placing fourth in the incredibly competitive World Cross Country Championships that fall. He is one of Athletics West's big success stories and is a great favorite of AW coach Bob Sevene, who had originally admired Porter's gutsy front-running style in the world meet.

Just about everybody in the business would be at the window right now cashing in some chips, but not Porter. He is faintly disdainful of the roads, and becomes almost apoplectic at the mention of the marathon.

"I don't want to even think about it much, but the marathon may end up being my best event," he says, sounding a little like a guy who just got a bad lab report back. "But I'm not going to go to it before I get every ounce out of myself in the five and ten on the track. What I really want to do is to win the World Cross Country Championship. To me that's every bit as important as winning a gold medal on the track. In Europe it's thought of that way. If you win the cross country title, you're thought of as the best distance runner in the world."

Which may seem like a strange and esoteric preoccupation to the average American connoisseur of the long distance run, until you remember that when he makes such pronouncements, Pat Porter is sitting smack dab in the middle of a mile and a half high desert, home to Saints and Madmen and Lost Tribes. And he says that though he doesn't plan to end up on Boot Hill here, he will stay for five years, or ten years, or however long it takes, abjuring the bright lights of more, uh, diverse aerobic communities, which at least around Alamosa can be summed up in one word: Boulder.

Oh, he's not exactly hurting. He has bought himself a nice little stucco house right off the campus, and he drives himself an almost new pick-up truck in the customary 4-wheel drive configuration (he has a beautifully restored '29 Model A in the garage), and he has a wall-sized projection television. But he is unquestionably turning down at least the $100,000 a year or so he could be making on the roads right now. All of which brings us directly to the Cinnamon Bun Metaphor:

Here is Porter, at the Campus Cafe at 8 in the morning, having just run six miles up seven-story *sand dunes*, speaking rapturously about winning titles that require one to thrash through 10,000 meters of mud, hills, hay bales and other interesting indignities. He is talking about how he will go to the roads to make some money only when the rest of it isn't working for him anymore. And as he talks he is methodically taking apart this giant pastry. With knife and fork, he very carefully starts on the outer ring, cutting off a piece at a time, working his way in, until after several minutes he is left with the prize: the perfect, round, completely cinnamon coated bulls-eye of the bun sitting in the middle of his plate, which he is now contemplating thoughtfully.

His guest asks, "Were you the kind of kid that saved the cherry until the rest of the ice cream sundae was gone?"

"Hey, yeah," he says, "Wonder what interesting psychological insight that provides."

"It's simple," says the guest. "You are a walking monument to deferred gratification."

"Wow," he says, looking a little troubled. "I never thought about that. Interesting." He starts to go on to something else, stops, brow wrinkled in thought. "Pretty interesting," he repeats.

Then he swoops on the cinnamon bulls-eye.

Adams State (student body around 2,000) is referred to fondly by friend and foe alike as "Taco Tech." New Mexico is just down the road. Picante sauce arrives whether you order it or not. It shouldn't surprise anyone that most G's are silent around here. The name is pronounced Vee-hill.

That applies to both Coach Joe Vigil and Charley Pablo

Vigil, who is no relation to the coach but who nevertheless ran for him a few years back. Charley still trains in Alamosa and these days is a world class *mountain* runner, but when Pat Porter arrived on campus he was simply the king bee. A sub-30-minute 10K runner and feared cross country competitor, Charley had been to the mountain top. Actually, he had been to Boulder. And he had spoken to, run with, broken bread with The Rojas. The Lindsay. The *Shorter.* Porter, needless to say, fresh from a school that didn't exist, was awed, and the two are fast friends and training partners yet.

It was Charley Pablo who invented the term, "Vee-hiloso-phy," an appropriate and useful phrase for the wisdom dispensed daily from the coach's beehive of an office in the Adams State gym.

Example: "You've got to eat as though you were a poor man. You've got to do endurance training daily. And you can't let your mind go to seed. I think if runners would observe these three things, they would have a complete life, in which they would get satisfaction from their world."

It is that sort of thing that so delights Charley Pablo and Pat Porter and the others who have been living and thriving in this rare atmosphere, in this astringent light for such a long time. Vigil is, as Porter puts it, "a good 'head' coach."

"I'm not saying he's the best coach in the world, but he's a darned good one. And for me he's the best in the world. He does so much more than just train your body. He trains your mind."

For his part Vigil is careful to downplay his influence: "Through the years I've seen Pat evolve as a sort of end result of my teaching philosophies, and yes, he's done it with hard work. He's always believed in me as a coach, and I feel a responsibility because of that. This two-way compassion we have for each other's roles has synergized into a good working situation for both of us. But I don't try to get into his mind when I'm not supposed to. I know that as a coach I have to be removed sometimes. There are times he has to think his own thoughts."

Porter, he says, still has his greatest races within him for three reasons. First, because "I haven't begun to play his weak suit yet . . ." Meaning, presumably, his speed. Second: "He hasn't really matured completely yet. By that I mean he hasn't tapped complete control." And third: "He has never been in the right situation to run a really good time for a 10K. He had one pretty good effort at Mt. Sac and ran 27:47, but he is still virtually a virgin on the track."

Nevertheless, Porter's performance this past cross country season makes Vigil think his student is ready to break through once and for all: "Bickford, Eyestone, and Nenow were the best around in the 10K, but when Pat can go out there and thrash them by 21 seconds . . . And I don't care what the conditions were, a race is a race is a race . . ."

And speaking of Bickford, et al., as distance coach for the next Olympics, Vigil is sanguine about overall US strength: "I believe we're entering an era when we have half a dozen runners of the highest caliber. Add Keith Brantly and Craig Virgin to Pat and the others and we have the greatest pool of distance runners in the world."

Vigil's training is based on how quickly the individual runner is trying to reach a peak. Those in it for the long haul are on a 14 day cycle, with more "easy" days between the hard days. Those doing it quick and dirty will be on the seven day cycle. Those going for the foreseeable future, a ten day cycle. As befitting a physiologist-coach, he tests all his runners for max VO2 and other variables. He says slyly: "I *like* to play the weak suit."

His college runners do between 75 and 85 miles a week in the fall. This past season Porter was doing 120. Vigil figures the altitude is worth a 20 percent differential. He believes in mileage:

"Volume to me is the single most important indicator in

the training regimen. It's not the only important one. Runners such as I have here will give me four to five hundred hours of training a year. When you get up to Pat's level, I've got to have 1,000 hours. He's operating on a different level. And in order for you to stimulate the training threshold level, he's got to train beyond the point that elicited the response the year before."

Seeking that threshold will regularly involve some truly amazing feats. The afternoon after his cinnamon bun breakfast Porter and a group of the undergraduates were scheduled for a 10-mile time trial. The first mile was under 4:40. They ran a familiar course away from campus and town, and in a matter of a few minutes they were in the desert, seemingly hell-bent for the mountains in the distance. Porter pulled gradually away from Charley Pablo, who slowly pulled away from the rest. One by one, they hit an invisible turn-around point and reversed direction, everyone obviously working hard. Porter came in just over 50 minutes, with Charley some 30 seconds behind. Then everybody was obliged to do a lot of serious knee-grabbing and air sucking.

Later that night Porter will meet Charley Pablo, wife Cindy and infant Noelle at—what else?—a Mexican restaurant for an evening's respite from the relentless 100-plus miles a week high altitude grind. The picante sauce will be brought whether ordered or not, and they will talk of races long run and companions long scattered. When they talk of races it will be of cross country, and mountain, and track races. The big city 10K's and marathons will be far away in mind as well as in geographical fact.

But for now Porter is not particularly happy about his 10-mile time trial: "In the past I've done that as fast as 47:30," he says, heading off to the training room to get some sound on his perennially sore plantar's.

Forty seven minutes and thirty seconds. In training. And forgive the repetition but again, this is still at lung-searing *altitude* we're talking about, a simple lack of oxygen that can make even phenomenally hardened athletes like Porter wince.

"I once did an all-out mile time trial up here," he says, eyes wide at the memory. "I ran a 4:01. I can't describe to you what that was like. I saw God."

Which is after all precisely what Saints and Madmen and Lost Tribes come seeking in the high desert.

May, 1986

Again to Carthage

There is a certain metaphorical symmetry in the infernal contraptions that we ride side by side, Frank Shorter and I, in the brightly-lit, mirror-glass-wood-grained interior of the Flatiron Athletic Club in Boulder.

These are the machines to which most of the walking wounded among long distance runners have been consigned at one time or another—some permanently it would seem—and whatever the beneficial effects of this kind of "alternate training," there is no question that at the heart of these beasts is a certain inherent futility: We are biking to nowhere.

"Oh, you get used to it," Frank says cheerfully. He has long since made his peace with the silly thing, as if in realization that such a coming-to-terms is a nonnegotiable prerequisite for an athlete on the comeback trail. You could almost believe that he would as soon be doing his morning "run" by cranking away on this upright coffee grinder as by taking an easy seven-miler in the mountains. But then you would recall his first experience with the futility-cycle after his ankle surgery in 1977. With one leg casted halfway to the knee, he would grimly point the thing toward a blank wall and grind out an hour on it without benefit of Walkman, VCR or window.

"I didn't want any diversions," he said. "I just wanted to make it as hard as I could." Since that time any number of world class types have made such a separate peace with the nowhere bike: Alberto Salazar, Joan Benoit, Mary Decker. Think of the most fleet and the most damaged.

If they have the item we seek, we will sooner or later come to an arrangement with our demons. Analysts of our culture are now confronted with growing numbers of former champions (and runner-ups and also-rans) who refuse to gracefully exit stage left. I am no exception.

In 1969, at the tender age of 22, I took precisely 4:06.7 to become the Southeastern Conference mile champion. I thought at the time that I could run quite a bit faster than that. I still do. I am on my 127th major comeback.

As a cultural phenomenon, the growing interest in coming back (as well as in never leaving in the first place) will all be dealt with in due time—if it hasn't already—in the pages of *Esquire, Harper's,* et al. We will no doubt be informed once again that the whole phenomena can be attributed to the fanatical self-absorption of us baby boomers. Which is fine. I hereby challenge the authors of such theories a race.

When the Los Angeles Olympics were looming, there were any number of declared and secret comeback efforts going on around the world, and if we didn't know about or take seriously many of them, that is perfectly consistent with the psychology of the comeback. We're talking about the real comeback now, and not repudiations of those little collective mental lapses in which, for example, several dozen sports writers decide that by dint of a couple of poor races Joan Benoit is ready for Century Village.

True comebacks—the kind that feature a veteran champion who has been dormant for a reasonable period of time—are not really supposed to succeed, and that is why the whole idea fills most of us with a kind of bittersweet romanticism. In the back of our minds we hold onto the disclaimer: Aw, he/she really is too old. Isn't he/she?

But there is something in us that wants desperately to believe that Ali could climb back in the ring with a much younger man and win the day once again. We rooted for Billy Jean King when she played some teenager during her umpteenth appearance on Center Court before the Queen.

And there is plenty of bona fide precedent for putting a few chips on the wise and wily veteran. Remember discuss man Al Oerter and his four clock-like returns to form and to Olympic gold from 1956 through 1972? Indeed, we shouldn't even be using the word "comeback" anymore. We should call them "oerters."

God knows, we *want* to believe in comebacks. Sylvester Stallone has taken that curious affinity and created an entire movie genre out of it. Some of it has to do with our soft spot for the familiar champion, comfortable as an old chair, who we were tricked by media fluffery into thinking we knew personally. Some of it is a natural tendency to root for the underdog. And a great deal of it is probably linked in some bizarre Adlerian way to our own personal quest for immortality.

Before the LA Games, if you listened carefully to those former champions scattered around the world undertaking comebacks of varying degrees of seriousness, you might have thought there were as many rationales for such endeavors as there were athletes. Lasse Viren told a reporter for *Running*: "They may think I am crazy, but I do not care a bit! Of course it might be wiser to stop when the time comes, but there are some things that annoy me. Finland's future in distance running doesn't look very bright. I think I may still offer them the best hope."

If he had made it to LA, it would have been 12 years since he won double golds in the 5,000 and the 10,000 at Munich, a feat he repeated four years later in Montreal, and then added a fifth place in the marathon a few days later. An injury hobbled him in Moscow in 1980, yet he managed a fifth in the 10K final anyway. But nationalism falls pretty low in the rankings of declared motivations for comebacks. One that seems to rate much higher is the burning desire to show any number of smug so-and-so's who have written you off just how completely,irrevocably, and publicly *wrong* they can be. Remember Sebastian Coe's vigorous gesture to the press after his 1,500 victory?

It has always mystified me how such naysayers—the press, insensitive friends, bemused relatives—can bank certain fires within us. Perhaps it is their incredibly complacent assumption that everyone they know—and most especially *you*—are doomed to the same mediocrity the see all around them. After some considerable success in sports, an athletic brand of *noblesse oblige* ought to arise and allow us to pardon such faint hearts.

With most of us, alas, it is not so. I can still very distinctly remember sitting in the gym bleachers in phys ed, chatting with a ninth-grade classmate about my plans for the coming school year. "I'm going out for the junior varsity basketball team," I said with some small measure of confidence. He looked at me with a mixture of pity and contempt and pronounced: "You won't make it."

But it was the *way* he said it that remains most vivid. Although he had not the slightest notion of my ability in the sport, he was just so *sure* that I was a dreamy idiot reaching for too-distant stars, and that he, on the other hand, was a realistic fellow with his feet firmly on the ground. His tone was so nettling that prickly hairs stood up on the back of my neck. I said nothing.

Over the years I often wondered if that 14-year-old even remembered the sentence of failure he was so willing to pronounce on an acquaintance. And if so, what must he have thought when the object of his scorn later won All-State honors and scholarship bids? Did it skew his world-view?

Benji Durden's entire road-racing career might be viewed as a comeback built upon such a remark.

"You'll never amount to anything. You're a quitter," pronounced Spec Townes, his college track coach, as the interval-weary runner turned in his spikes. It is difficult to imagine an athletic assessment being more clearly wrong-headed.

"He deserves a lot of credit for what I've accomplished by saying that to me. And I mean that sincerely," Durden said shortly after winning two marathon purses and banking exactly $40,000.

"I guess he's proved his point," Townes finally sighed, a few years back.

Nick Rose said that being written off by track & field *cognoscenti* proved to be a great incentive in training for England's team for Helsinki. "There was a period of time I went through when I was injured and trying to come back and it made it worse when people would say: 'Oh, you're not going to do it.' That was quite hard to deal with. Deep down inside I knew I could." Even Viren, when asked what the prime motivating force for a comeback would be, said: "Well, there is something left [to prove]: To show those people who secretly—and even publicly—are thinking, 'Viren is finished, he will do nothing worthwhile any more.' Just to show them."

Such are the kind of sentiments to get one through the last several miles of a hard Sunday 20-miler, or the final burning set of an interval workout, perhaps.

But there is another, gentler reason many dormant athletes take to the field once more—or refuse to relinquish it in the first place. Though it would very difficult for someone who has never been an athlete on some kind of organized team to understand, I think a lot of us just want to make the traveling squad again.

Peter Gent, a former pro football player and the author of *North Dallas Forty*, addressed that point nicely in a piece he wrote not long ago about Mickey Mantle in retirement. The baseball legend, Gent reported, liked to spend most of his time hanging around the clubhouse of his golf course:

"I like it, too," wrote Gent. "The clubhouse does have the quality of an elegant locker room, which is like a kind of methadone for former athletes. I can feel it myself and sense what he must find soothing about it. It ain't the real thing, but you can take some measure of comfort in it."

I tried to capture something of the same feeling in describing the training table of a jock dorm in my novel, *Once A Runner:*

> "Several dozen athletes screamed, laughed, cajoled and punched each other in the easy fond intimacy which sports give to young men in groups and which they would consciously or subconsciously miss during the rest of their lives. . ."

At the time of the Lake Tahoe high-altitude trials for the Mexico City Olympics in 1968, you could read little stories from time to time about some of the big names from days gone by who were up at Lake Tahoe giving it another shot. Billy Mills, who had won the gold in the 10,000 in Tokyo; Bob Schul, who had won the 5,000 the same year; Gerry Lindgren, who had won almost everything *but* an Olympic medal, and who later went into hiding. You could almost sense their attitude from the stories: They didn't really expect they could do much of anything at the Games, they just wanted to be a part of it all again.

"So much of distance training just seems to be water under the bridge," sighed Billy Mills at the time. Such is not the sentiment of someone likely to go out and beat everyone in the world. Yet there must be something haunting and powerful in the echoing drip of a solitary showerhead in a deserted locker room. Something powerful enough to bring proud, former champions back hat-in-hand from the comfort of home and kids and encroaching middle age.

This was the sentiment I think Frank Shorter was getting at when he told me: "You have to do it for no ulterior motive. You have to do it for the thing itself." Which is very much what one would expect the thoughtful, illusion-less Shorter to say.

Whenever you talk to an athlete who once returned to active competition after a good while away—and it hardly mat-

ters with what success—you often sense a truly mystified pleasure in their athletic rebirth. It is as if, once having ventured
out into the real world of blurred values and ambiguous finish
lines, he had thought to be banned forever from this other, this
far more clearly defined sphere.

Bob Sevene, an early member of the Billy Squires/Rodgers
Boston running Mafia, now coach of Bowdoin and Benoit, felt
that way about his return to competition after a tour in
Vietnam:

"I can remember in 1974, the year of the gas shortage,
chipping in our money to go down to New York on the train to
run the two-mile relay against Chicago Track Club. That was
the year they broke the world record. Greater Boston Track
Club was just getting started then. We had great duels with
them. Hell, *we* were old men, *they* were old men. I mean,
Walhutter wasn't old, but Sparks, Lowell Paul . . . we were
antiques out there on the track.

"But we broke the world record in the Garden in the TAC
and just barely got beat by them. I had as much fun that year as
I had had in 1967. Billy Squires began to coach us, we picked
up some younger runners, and of course there was Billy
Rodgers. It was a great group. That was really a second running
career for me. I wasn't that great, but I was running as good as I
ever did. And it was just flat, flat *fun*."

Or as elite master Cindy Dalrymple told *The Runner*
about her return to form after a 10-year hiatus: "I wouldn't give
this up for anything."

But no one pays for such fun like the athlete coming back.
Dalrymple described her first few weeks: "It was awful. I started
out running for a while, then just quit. I felt tired, I thought I
was too old. I ran my first race after two weeks of jogging. I did
35 minutes for five miles and thought I was going to die."

The irony of comeback training is the frustration inherent
in *remembering* when it was all so much easier. "Anyone who
has made a marathon comeback—whether from illness, injury
or layoff—knows the feeling: days of sluggishness, when lazy

muscles are asked to be active again; weeks of gradual increas-
es, when a 10-mile run is ultradistance and a 20-miler is impossible; months of planning, when the long-term goal seems a
fuzzy dream, too near to prepare for or too distant to be rele-
vant; and moments of despair when the time and effort spent
seem out of proportion to the projected rewards," wrote
Olympian Don Kardong of his own painful return to sub-2:20
shape.

Doone Riley, of Prince George, British Columbia, ran her
first real race in a long time at the Tulsa Run in October, 1983.
She had broken 3:00 in the marathon in 1978, but had been
completely away from running for two years.

"There is a certain amount of pressure on you," she said.
"You have people who remember you from when you were a
good runner, and then all of a sudden you are coming back,
you're at the back of the pack and they say: Oh, what's wrong
with you? The classic example was one terrible race I had.
When I finally made it back to the finish line, one official said:
'What happened to you? Did you get lost?' That's pressure."

"Paying some real dues," is what two-time Olympian Jack
Bacheler called the process, struggling back from several years
of serious injury problems for a shot at masters competition.
"But I think most of us, if we could remove ourselves from the
normal pressures of job, family and so on and do nothing but
eat right and think about training, would surprise ourselves by
the improvement we could make."

"You've got to be a little bored to be doing really good
training," Marty Liquori once told me. "Your training runs have
to become the focal point of your day." Most of us who are well
advanced into adulthood dream about finding that kind of simplicity again, but rarely do.

Viren told an interviewer: "The secret . . . is enjoying the
hard grind of everyday training. And when you are getting
older there are so many other things in life that are trying to
take the place of it."

The familiarity of those familiar worn handholds can be

both blessing and curse on the long climb back up the mountain. When you've just turned your soul inside out to finish 20 quarters in 75 seconds each, it probably doesn't do you much good to remember a happier day when they would have been 10 seconds faster. Shorter says he finds such reference points comforting. Doone Riley said she'd rather not know.

"The first time you ever run five miles, it's a real high," she said. "But the first time you run five miles in a comeback, it hurts. You think: I used to be able to run a marathon, and now five miles is killing me. It's very depressing." How true, dear Doone.

We all long for happy endings to comeback stories, yet we sooner or later come to grips with reality. Dame Fate reserves as much disappointment for veterans grimly struggling back as she does for wide-eyed first-timers. Neither Mills, nor Schul, nor Lindgren made it to the Olympics in 1968.

And much as we all want to make the traveling squad once again, we also know that there is a delicately balanced formula within each of us that determines the precise point at which it is no longer worth it. A strand of gristle goes pop and we throw up our hands in despair once more.

Yet even then the injuries fade, the spirit itself heals. And something draws us back. Lindgren, coaxed out of hiding by Kenny Moore, is back running road races under his own name. Bacheler found a doctor who knew what was wrong with his hip and was soon doing up to 70 a week. Rudy Chapa came back from virtual obscurity to run 2:11 for seventh at New York a few years back. Antonio Villanueva returns after several dormant years and runs 2:13 as a master.

And sweet, illusion-less Frank Shorter happily grinds away on his futility-cycle, dreaming dreams of coming again to Carthage.

April, 1984

Exit the Dragon

Consider for a moment the cruel sort of introspection visited upon the hard-charging urban runner-jock by one world class athlete by the name of Gary Fanelli, who, for grins, likes to dress up in a Blue Brothers suit—complete with cheap sunglasses—and cruise a 10K roadrace in, oh, around 32 minutes. To the runner who for months has faithfully done his intervals, his stretching, his Sunday 20- miler, who believes in God, country and Shearson-American Express, and who has been thereby (he believes) closing in on the dreaded 34-minute barrier, Fanelli's idea of fun must intimate a universe gone awry.

It is one of the grimmer realities of the sport that someone who can run a 10K foot race in 29 minutes in racing nylon, can, without undue strain, cover the same distance in 33 minutes in a suit of armor. Or pushing his eight-month-old infant in a buggy. Or balancing a bottle of Perrier and a couple of glasses on a waiter's tray.

This whole Mardi Gras approach to road racing apparently began, as have so many of our nation's collective psychic hiccups, on the West Coast, many years ago in the infamous Bay to Breakers race. Nowadays any serious runners reckless enough to show up there are overwhelmed by hordes of galloping bunny rabbits, gorillas, Count Draculas, and, of course, multi-membered convict chain gangs, and insects of various descriptions.

Notwithstanding the damaged egos of those who must glumly report that they finished "behind the centipede," I have always considered such stunt running to be harmless enough. It might even furnish an adequate and amusing alibi for the level-headed jogger looking to downplay the competitive aspects of the sport while still taking part in races: "Sure, I finished 9,728th. How fast do you think a guy can run dressed like a shepherd?"

The idea of my own participation in such chicanery, however, has been an improbability of such proportions that no hyperbole would suffice to inform the reader. Let us say simply that the idea never crossed my mind.

It did however, cross the demented mind of my friend and neighbor, Steve Pfeiffer (and yes, he insists that you pronounce, or try to pronounce it with a "p"). A grinning, blond, impish sort of fellow, his train of thought steams off in such unpredictable directions that in an earlier era I would not have been surprised to find him a full fledged Merry Prankster on Ken Kesey's psychedelic cross-country bus ride. I would not, in fact, have been surprised to find him behind the wheel.

It so happens that Steve, who several years ago witnessed a Bay to Breaker race, has a brother, Jay—an equally grinning, blond and impish fellow, who happens to have certain practical engineering skills that allow a percentage of his younger sibling's schemes to come to fruition. Also, being the proprietor of a small farm, he owns a bunch of irrigation tubing. Which is to say that it was Jay Pfeiffer who actually built the damned dragon and I believe any jury in this country would find him equally culpable. But I am getting ahead of my story. (Actually, from a strictly legal standpoint, my participation in this ludicrous and painful affair falls into the category of what lawyers call "Assumption of Risk," which is what the judge tells you after you volunteer to wrestle the Kodiak bear at the county fair and you end up with your front end slightly out of alignment.)

Anyway, this whole improbable affair began with an innocent-sounding message on my phone-answering machine. It was Marsha, Steve's charming and amazingly tolerant wife, who sounded altogether too giggly and tentative: "Hey, John, when you and Mary Ann get in, why don't you come on over. Steve wants to talk to you about, uh, sort of running a race with him and some friends this weekend . . ."

I could hear some raucous Pfeiffer-brother cackling in the background before she hung up, which should have been warning enough for anyone in full control of his faculties. I, however had been tapped ever so gently by the Budweiser Fairy that night. Thus we shortly found ourselves in the Pfeiffer living room listening to what began to shape up as an increasingly sound idea to run 6.2 miles with the deranged Pfeiffer brothers while toting several hundred pounds of irrigation tubing and painted Styrofoam fashioned into the ostensible shape of a mythological beast. They had already found two recruits, Martha Nebelseick and Rick Budell, whose motives remain to me to this day a complete mystery. I don't remember much about how they talked me into it, but I do remember little snatches of dialogue that indicate I wasn't exactly easy to negotiate with:

PFEIFFER BROTHER (I don't recall which): We had originally planned to have some kind of voluptuous cave-woman type female run out in front, leading the dragon on a leash. But person such as that tend not to be in very good aerobic shape.

PARKER: They also tend to be spoken for.

PFEIFFER: Good point.

PARKER: Look, have you thought about how other runners will take this? How would *you*, for instance, like to be beaten by a dragon?

PFEIFFER: We won't be passing anyone. No one's gonna get humiliated.

PARKER: No one but us.

PFEIFFER: Here's another thing. You'll be in front, so you can set the pace.

PARKER: Fine. How's 5:45 sound?

PFEIFFER: That would give our dragon a very awkward shape.

PARKER: Hey, fellows, seriously, couldn't you just find someone else? This is not exactly my cup of tea.

PFEIFFER: Parker, I don't want to hurt your feelings, but you were not exactly our first choice. The fact of the matter is we had some last-minute cancellations. Edie Williams, for instance, called to say her husband wouldn't let her run six miles in a dragon suit with three other guys . . .

This went on for a while. Finally Steve said, "Look, it's going to happen with you or without you." This had the far-off ring of Kesey's Merry Prankster truism: "You're either *on* the bus, or you're *off* the bus."

My wife, Mary Ann, a no-nonsense Missouri farm girl, had been watching this process with a sort of wry fatalism. She knew which way the wind was blowing.

"Come on, Puff," she said to me, "Time for bed."

I believe I can sum up the race itself fairly succinctly.

The first point I would like to make is that offensive personal habits become greatly magnified inside a dragon suit. A word to the wise.

The second point I would like to make can be stated as a sort of axiom of physics: Any lighthearted idea that entails carrying several tons of irrigation equipment on your shoulders for long distances on a hot Florida spring morning becomes geometrically less amusing after the first, say, 200 yards or so.

A sociological observation: Despite the best efforts of your most creative costume designers, 19 percent of the American spectating public will insist or referring to your standard 10,000 meter dragon as a "lizard."

Practical advice: When selecting dragon teammates, try to maintain a certain height consistency. I am a somewhat taller-than-average individual, so you can imagine how hurt my feelings were when, at about the four-mile mark, I turned gaspingly around and could swear I saw Martha Nebelseick's little Nikes just sort of gently dragging along the ground.

On the competitive instinct: In the latter stages of a race, when a well-paced dragon begins to launch into its sustained and brutal kick, you *will* see some panic stricken sprints by flagging competitors. For naught, I happily add.

The dragon ran 66:15 and thereby created a truly memorable kind of watershed. For years hence folks around here will be discussing the 1985 Springtime Tallahassee race in terms of whether they finished "before the dragon" or "after the dragon."

And despite whatever differences may have arisen beneath our green outer covering, there was no question that a certain *esprit-de-dragon* had formed among our little green-legged band. As we staggered around congratulating each other afterwards, it was apparent that the four taller members had even forgiven the diminutive Martha Nebelseick for swinging from her hand grips, a truly nefarious habit that she denied to the end.

After a time, a haggard looking Steve Pfeiffer stumbled over to where Mary Ann was ministering to me. He put his hand on my thoroughly bruised shoulder, looked me in the eye and said: "You know, Parker, it wasn't until about the quarter-mile mark that the gravity of what we had undertaken truly settled on me."

"I know, Steve, I felt the same way," I said, wiping some of the stinging sweat our of my eyes.

"Maybe now," said the ever-wise Mary Ann, "you'll have more respect for those guys in penguin suits."

And she's right, I do. Because even though we clearly finished first in the mythological beast division, we were about twenty minutes behind a guy and his wife pushing their kid in a stroller.

July, 1985

Smoke and Mirrors:
Why Jim Fixx Really Died

I have just gone through a large stack of my least-favorite running magazine, looking for articles I might want to save before pitching the lot. The pickings were, as expected, pretty humble. We needn't name names here, suffice it to say that my least-favorite running magazine has been around for quite awhile and usually features a cover shot of a smiling 22-year-old female model doing some bizarre and essentially useless stretching routine (they seem to have this thing about dining room chairs). Or else a nice close-up of a spoonful of wheat germ.

Almost every issue seems to contain an article on "Runner's High," and most editions contain other sly "Secrets" you might employ to gain an advantage over your competition—all the while positively disdaining the very *idea* that anyone would actually want to achieve something as crass as beating another human being in an athletic contest. This publication thus retains at its very core an abiding contradiction that its editors have never even understood, much less addressed.

Some typical article titles are: "The Role of the B Vitamins in Daily Life," "Yoga and Running Make a Very Good Partnership," "Boots Are Made for Running: There Are Shortcuts to Leg Strength," "Zen, Childbirth and the Running Stitch," and "Is It the Right Time for Milk?" (This last uses as an illustration a headbanded and very troubled looking runner staring directly into the eyes of the fiercest looking moo-cow I've ever seen.)

One such article, entitled "Herbs: Next to his Shoes, the Runner's Best Friend May Be in the Kitchen" has provided me with a joke I always use when I speak at race clinics: " . . . after I read the article I tried rubbing sassafras into my quads for a couple of weeks. I don't know if it helped my running any, but when I boiled my shorts it made a pretty nice tea . . ."

Which is a more helpful suggestion than you'll find in any given issue of my least favorite running magazine.

All of this is by way of an oblique approach to a subject you probably don't want to hear any more about and about which I am not particularly excited myself, which is the death of Jim Fixx.

Before rolling your eyes and bagging this whole thing, let me explain that the only reason I feel compelled to trod this too-well-worn ground behind all the sport's pundits and wire-service Thinkers is that in all the millions of words written along the lines of "What-Will-This-All-Mean-to-Running" and "He-Would-Have-Died-Sooner-If-He-Hadn't-Been-A-Runner" and "He-Died-For-What-He-Believed-In," everyone, and I mean *everyone*, completely missed the essential truth of Fixx's death, which is simply that Jim Fixx was never really the person the American public believed him to be.

I never met him, but from mutual friends I have it that he was a fine fellow, as friendly and personable as you could ask, and not the least bit haughty from his success. But he was set up as a straw man Guru of Aerobic Excellence and when he died all the pundits and Thinkers were immediately in a dither as to what it all meant. In point of fact it didn't mean anything except the sad death of one man.

In the late sixties and early seventies I lived, trained, and competed with some very serious long distance runners, runners whose abilities were amply demonstrated in ways that simply preclude debate: they won national championships, they won international championships. They won, in fact, Olympic medals. I didn't know a single one of them, even way back then, who didn't consider my least favorite running magazine to be a long-standing joke, a monthly compendium of trendy fluff for the kind of dilettante who desperately wants to believe that you can accomplish difficult things by rubbing something on your body, taking the right kind of capsule, or by stretching interminably on your living room carpet.

It told us a great deal about Jim Fixx—and the fitness "boom" in general—to find out that he considered my least favorite running magazine to be a veritable fount of useful information.

And it tells you a lot about our culture to realize that in this one realm of endeavor—long distance running—where ability can be accurately and objectively measured in unambiguous black and white numbers, in this one tiny crucible where there is no way to dress your way to success, politic your way past less devious colleagues, or bullshit your way to accomplishment, that most people chose to believe that Jim Fixx was a great runner despite the clear evidence of his own performances to the contrary. The dust jacket of his first book noted that he had competed in "and finished" six Boston Marathons, but doesn't tell us whether it took him two hours or two days. The truth of the matter is that Jim Fixx required a good deal more than forty minutes to complete a 10,000-meter foot-race. His best marathon time was three hours and twelve minutes. These are performances nowadays honorably claimed by any number of grandmothers.

There is, alas, no place to hide in this particular athletic arena. There is only one criterium, and it is as cold, cruel and as *effective* a standard of ability as anything you'll find in this life. If you hold yourself out to have special knowledge or abili-

ty in running, I need only look to your performances in black
and white numbers to see in an instant if you deserve my attention and respect or if you are, in fact, a pretender. Of course,
one might have special knowledge in a field without being able
to prove it personally, as in the case of the great editor who is
not a great writer. In running, such people are called coaches.
But again, to judge a coach's ability I need only look to the performances of his or her athletes. Period.

Jim Fixx coached no athletes and his personal perfor-
mances firmly entrenched him in the ranks of mediocrity. He
was no expert at all.

I say this not to be cruel or superior, but to point out a simple truth far more important than what Fixx's death means to
the fitness craze: As a society we have an affinity for the ersatz
that may well be the end of us. Just as an individual who cannot distinguish between internal and external reality is said to
be schizophrenic, a culture that cannot distinguish between
images and reality is in precipitous decline.

This is not to say that Fixx didn't play a role in getting
many people involved in an essentially healthy activity, but the
truth of the matter is that Fixx was more of a product of the
running boom than vice versa. The movement really started in
1972 when Frank Shorter won the Olympic marathon; nearly
anyone could have come along and written the essential hand-
book for joggers, and in fact probably could have done so years
earlier (our image packagers do nothing so well as to spot a
trend that has been staring them directly in the eyeball). Had
he remained a journeyman guide helping complete novices
explore new and exciting territory, he might have been all
right, but Fixx's role, as was completely predictable, became
much more than that of a Pied Piper.

As one essayist was perplexed at how someone like Gloria
Steinem could be relentlessly referred to as "a writer" despite
her never having written much of anything to speak of, the ele-
vation of Jim Fixx to Aerobic Guru despite his complete lack of
anything resembling a background for it is a metaphor for the

epistemological confusion of our times. We are *beset* by experts without portfolio.

The process by which this happens is instructive: On our two latitudinal coasts are our twin image factories, New York and Los Angeles, where on any given workday a relative handful of bright, ambitious, and over-stimulated men and women spend far too much time on the telephone and at lunch with other each deciding which trends look profitable and which images might be employed in the packaging and sale of those trends to the American public.

Ironically, Jim Fixx had in fact been a part of that image factory, as an overweight, hard smoking, hard lunching magazine editor in New York. He eventually became a runner and broke away from that world. But he still knew its customs and folkways, and he still had his contacts.

If the publishing industry in New York were the least bit interested in authenticity, *The Complete Book of Running* would have been written by Hal Higdon, who, at age 54 is a long-time excellent athlete as well as fine writer on the subject, or by Joe Henderson, a runner of some accomplishment and the one editor who long gave my least favorite running magazine whatever credibility it may have had.

But it was Fixx who put "the deal" together, and that is where it all happens these days: "the deal." It was Fixx who packaged America's aerobic fantasy for mass consumption, and when he signed that publishing contract with Random House, his fate was sealed. There was never a better example of the wrong guy in the right place at the right time.

This is not to say he was some kind of blatant self-promoter. In fact he probably never personally claimed to have been much of an expert on running. He didn't really have to. The image factory took care of that for him. He would appear at race clinics and, while sitting on the very stage with Olympic medalists, learned coaches, and 12-year-old age group whizzes who could outrun him in shower thongs, people in the audience would ask *Jim Fixx* what he thought about training. They would ask him what stretching routines he used, whether there were any shortcuts to leg strength, and if the time was right for milk. And whereas all those razor-thin athletes on the stage with Fixx would answer such questions with a shrug and simple, unsatisfying advice like "train your guts out," Fixx always seemed to have a lot of helpful hints on matters like "breathing correctly," diet, and shoe models. As he talked the athletes would trade secret, puzzled smiles.

The great unspoken suspicion in the audience must have been that all those runners with those unfathomable numbers to their credit (a 10K time that begins with the numeral "2"?) must know The Secret, but were too shy or selfish to articulate it. Fixx, on the other hand, always had suggestions. Never mind that the numbers next to his name were embarrassingly similar to ours, he wrote *the book,* for crying out loud.

Fixx knew better. He had been around running long enough to know precisely where his ability placed him in the scheme of things. But after many thousands come to you seeking wisdom and many thousands depart satisfied by what you have told them, you may well come to believe that you have wisdom to impart. I believe Fixx bought into his own myth, that he truly came to think of himself as an expert, a hardcore long term athlete, rather than a middle-aged, sedentary, high-stress urban American male who took up jogging late in life, thought he had found physical absolution, and wrote a book about it. Hardcore athletes, he must have figured, don't need stress tests. Fixx *actively* avoided taking one. Most of us would rather believe in the Wizard, and not go poking around for the little man behind the smoke and mirrors pulling the strings and levers. Fixx was his own little man behind the smoke and mirrors.

But a true endurance athlete is the ultimate realist. There is enough of a taste of death in a gut-searing interval workout to intimate very clearly our own mortality. Nonetheless, many of the athletes I ran with long ago are still training and competing at a high level, some breaking records almost as I write. We trained hard because we were athletes who wanted to win foot-races. If you want to undertake such a difficult task, you must be true to yourself and not create myths and excuses. It is a hard enough thing to do without cluttering it up with false notions. We did not run for "runner's high," fret over our diet, or spend any time stretching with dining room chairs.

Not a single one of us ever ran a step to improve our health, to strengthen our hearts, to cut a trim figure. That is what those shy, razor thin athletes on the stage with Jim Fixx were trying to tell people, but nobody wanted to listen. We had not the slightest doubt—still don't—that we were among the healthiest people in the world, but that was never our goal at all. It was the fire, not the smoke, we were after, in the words of Tom Robbins.

And thus, as the Zen archer taught, the arrow pierces the precise center of the target we were not aiming for at all. I don't know if this is comprehensible to those hard driving lunch-goers who yet toil in the image factories of LA and New York, but it is high time someone made an attempt to inform them of the subtle but insidious role their ersatz world played in the death of a congenial and well-meaning fellow.

Jim Fixx died from All American hype.

March, 1985

Well, it really hit the fan when this appeared in Ultrasport, *as you might imagine. The magazine printed several hot-under-the-collar retorts, as well as a very nice letter of support and agreement from Kenny Moore. A number of people, including a former editor of my least-favorite running magazine, seemed to think I was criticizing Fixx for not being an elite runner. Of course, that was not the case at all.*

Fixx's death was indeed a tragedy. But it was far from a mystery. Much more puzzling to me were the mysterious deaths of elite runners Stign Jaspers and Jeff Drenth, both of whom were is excellent competitive running shape when they succumbed. Jaspers was said to have had a rare congenital heart defect. They couldn't find anything at all wrong with Jeff. They now attribute his death to an electrical disturbance of the heart. His coach at Athletics West, Bob Sevene, to this day can't talk about it without breaking down. Jeff had died in his arms.

Funny, I read this piece now and I find myself as convinced as ever of its essential truth.

A Study in Brown

It was twilight and a small group of fit-looking runners was making the last nervous preparations around the starting line of the University of Florida's track in Gainesville. They were mostly undergraduate track team types, with several older, serious looking runners tagging along. It was easy to tell they were getting ready to do a hard interval workout because there was palpable tension and a trace of fear in their good-natured banter.

Bruce League, 32, a transplant from upstate New York and a 29-minute 10K runner, made the usual obligatory remark about the Gainesville training weather: "Well, boys, here it is December 18th and we're going *without* T-shirts again."

The breaking out of racing spikes for the occasion inspired familiar comments that generally went something like "Man, the last time I had these on was Penn Relays and . . . ."

Barry Brown looked up from lacing his shoes, a look of concentration furrowing his brow, as if trying to remember something. "The last time I had on these spikes, I believe, was the Olympic Games of 1896," he said.

No humor goes over quite so well as restating the obvious, and the newly-turned 40-year-old Brown's remark was received by the younger runners appreciatively. Finally, with spikes laced tightly and last minute bathroom trips taken care of, no one could think of any more reasons to stall around. The light-hearted comments were replaced by silence as they began to gather around the starting post. Brown said quietly to League: "Dark beer and lasagna for dinner tonight, if that's any incentive." Teague's eyebrows arched with interest.

A quarter mile running track is no place to expect deference for simple longevity. As Barry Brown began moving with his smooth, mechanical stride on the all-weather surface in the twilight, he began demonstrating once again why most knowledgeable observers feel he is not only going to rewrite the masters record books but also redefine our notions of athletic competitiveness and aging along the way.

After some warm-up sprints, he ran: a mile in 4:26, quarter jog; three half-miles in 2:14, 2:12, 2:09, quarter jog after each; and three quarter-miles in 62+, 61+, and 60.5. He was in the front of every repetition. With the warm-up, warm-down, and his eight miles that morning, he had put in over 20 miles that day, not unusual mileage for him.

"Not bad," he said, getting into his sweats. "I didn't really feel it until the last quarter when I got up on my toes . . ."

Barry Brown has already caused quite a stir in masters running, and there is every indication that he has just scratched the surface. In the first six months of his 40th year he:

• Won the world Veterans Championship 10,000 in San Diego with a 30:25 (a time he called "disappointing")

• Set a new American masters 10K record in the 4th Annual Asbury Park, NJ Classic in August with a 29:57

• Set an American masters record in the half marathon in the Maple Leaf half marathon in 1:06:24

• Set an American 8K masters record in the Strohs Run for Liberty in Gainesville in 24:15

• Ran an American record and personal best marathon time of 2:15:14 in the Twin Cities Marathon in Minneapolis

• Ran an unofficial two-mile world masters record on the

track in 9:06

And he's just not even trying hard yet. He picked up the American 20-mile record en route in the Twin Cities marathon. And the two-mile time was run on a high school track and was just part of his training day.

"Four days after I turned 40 I went to a little all-comers meet at my high school, just for a workout. It was my third workout of the day. The old record was 9:07.4 by somebody in Great Britain, which is ridiculously slow. I ran a 9:06, but it probably won't count because the track doesn't have a two-inch unbroken curve on the inside. The reason it doesn't bother me that much is I'll probably run 8:40 or so this year."

In the past, the best men's masters have tended to fall into two categories: those who took up running relatively late and discovered a latent talent, and those who had been competitive college runners, retired after graduation, and came back after a hiatus. Mike Manley, the first sub-30 minute masters runner, gave us a hint of what continually training world class competitor might achieve as a master, but he has had chronic injury problems, as has Bill Stewart, another masters record holder with credentials as a collegiate track performer.

Despite the fact he races often—sometimes every weekend for long stretches—Barry Brown seems to have solved much of the injury riddle. Perhaps his secret is the fact that he keeps the renowned trainer Brady Greathouse on full-time retainer. At any rate he is arguably at the forefront of a whole "new breed" of masters who have trained and competed at a national and international level straight through from his high school days. He makes only the slightest concessions to chronological age in training: interval workouts are approached carefully, but he is not at all a "light" trainer. 100-plus mile weeks are the norm with him.

"I get one long run, usually a 20-miler, on Sunday. Then I get a semi-long run, usually 15, on Wednesday. I try to get two interval workouts, or fartlek type workouts, one with shorter repetitions, one with longer—like repeat miles. I like to do repeat miles every other week just to see where I am. I've averaged 4:35 for seven with a quarter jog. The days in between are just easy runs 7-10 miles. And eight every morning, of course," he said.

But perhaps more noteworthy than his consistent high level training is the fact that he's not simply holding on, giving ground grudgingly to Father Time, he's actually *improving*, and believes he can still set PR's at everything from the 10K on up, including a marathon in the 2:10 range.

"I tease Barry a lot about setting p.p.'s at 40," chuckled long-time friend and fellow Gainesville resident Marty Liquori. "I told him, 'Barry, the reason you have kept improving over the years is that you started out so slow that there was a lot of *room* for improvement. If you had run a four minute mile in high school like I did, you would have run out of new territory to conquer pretty quickly.' "

He may not have run a four minute mile in high school, but to many who have followed his remarkable career, Barry Brown continues to be what he has been all along: something of a phenomenon. "You should see the way people treat him in Glens Falls," said League. "He's considered a legend up there."

At Colonie Central High in Albany he was merely good (4:28 in the mile, 9:48 in the two-mile). At Brown University, he won the NCAA indoor two-mile as a junior in 1965 with an 8:58, ended with college PR's of 4:05 and 8:53. He kept improving as he trained while in law school in Albany under the tutelage of Joe McClusky, bronze medalist in the 1936 Olympic steeplechase. The "steeple" was very much a stepchild in American track & field circles in those days, and Barry's 8:40 in his third attempt ever made him one of the country's best performers and marked the beginning of his career as an internationalist.

"At the Olympic high altitude training camp at Lake Tahoe in 1968, I became very much influenced by Pete Petersen, who was then coach of the California Striders. Jack Bacheler was very much taken by him as well, as was Marty and a number of other runners," said Brown. "Being pretty much self-coached after college, I had always been of the school that says you go out and run every workout as hard as you can, even the long runs. Pete was our introduction to the 'train, don't strain' approach, where you stay relaxed, keep your form, and train consistently that way, day after day. Training with him I got faster than I'd ever been, but without doing a lot of sprinting, and I got stronger than I'd ever been, without doing all that much mileage. I still think Pete was one of the best coaches I've ever met."

When, at the behest of then University of Florida head track coach Jimmy Carnes (later US Olympic coach and founder of Athletic Attic), Barry finally arrived in Gainesville in 1971 to make a serious attempt at the US team for the Munich Olympics, he fell in again with fellow Petersen-devotee Bacheler, and became part of the Florida Track Club dynasty of early 70's, along with Frank Shorter, Jeff Galloway, Sam Bair and others. Although he missed making the Olympic teams of '72 and '76, he was consistently one of the country's top performers, making a total of 20 US international teams over his career.

But Brown maintains his best performances are still ahead of him.

"I'd like to make all the world masters records—with the exception of Foster's 2:11 marathon—respectable. Foster's mark, of course, is already respectable. In fact, it's sort of 'Beamonesque.' Beyond that, I want to set PR's for everything from the 10K on up," he said.

"I hate the marathon," he admitted. He has good reason. In the 1976 Olympic trials he was running powerfully with Shorter and Rodgers right through the 18th mile, when complete dehydration surprisingly forced him to drop out. "I felt fine," he said, "I just couldn't move my legs." Don Kardong came on to take the third spot on the team. The marathon seems to tantalize him like that, always holding the prize out infuriatingly, then snatching it away at the last second. It never beats him in the normal way with sheer fatigue, but always with tricks.

"Minnesota proved to me that I could get through one relatively unscathed. But even then because of a cramp I couldn't run the last two or three miles hard enough to get tired. The next day I was able to go out and do 10 miles, then 16 the day after that. The way I look at it, my ultimate marathon potential can be extrapolated from my 30K PR, which was 4:54 per mile for 18.6 miles. If I could sustain that for 26.2 miles, it would come out to a 2:09:46 marathon. Of course, you would slow down some the last eight miles, but I don't think a well-conditioned marathoner would totally hit the wall.

"I look at Ron Tabb or Benji [Durden], and I don't think either one of those guys is any more talented than I am, and probably no faster over 10K. I think if they can run in the 2:09's under good conditions at Boston, then I should be able to run 2:10 under good conditions at Boston. I raced Tabb a lot of times at 10 miles and less and beaten him almost every time. With the marathon, I think it's just a question of running enough of them so that sooner or later you get the perfect day where everything goes right. On the other hand, running a lot of them is dangerous for injuries. It's a fine line. I hate the marathon," he repeated.

His attitude towards racing performances is that of the traditional track athlete: Winning by itself is not enough. He is only satisfied by what he knows himself to be a superior effort.

"Losing doesn't bother me as much as it used to, and it never really sent me into the depths of depression. Winning is the same way, really. I'm not exhilarated just to win. If I can get into a race even though I know I'm going to get beaten, but that I'll probably get a PR, I want to be in that race. If I can keep improving or stay at a respectable level, I'll run against anybody anywhere. That's why I'm not satisfied to just run masters races. It would be too easy just to do that and win easily. I'd rather run a 28:45 and get beat than to win the world master championships by 40 seconds in 30:25."

Asked if the traditional "good master" runner has a chance against the likes of a Barry Brown, he doesn't dilly dally with false modesty:

"No. But there are some guys to watch out for in Europe, where masters running is a lot bigger than it is here. I'm seeing guys now cropping up in the European results who I used to run against internationally. Alan Rushmore, from Great Britain, who was a bronze medalist in the Commonwealth Games, is now running masters. I saw one race where he ran 30:11 for 10K, a lot faster than anyone here is running, except me. Tim Johnston, an internationalist from England is running the 10K. Gunter Milke, who was an internationalist from West Germany. I think that's where my major competition is going to come from." The only current American masters Brown considers a potential threat is Mike Manley, like Brown a former internationalist in the steeplechase. "Mike and I could have some great races if he could stay healthy. But he's always hurt. He gets hurt, retires, comes back, retires again. But he's run 29:35 on the roads. Even if the course was uncertified, you've got to respect that," he said.

Old friend and teammate Jack Bacheler, now a professor at North Carolina State, knows something of the injury problems that seem to plague older runners. After turning 40 in 1983 he ran several good races, including a masters second place to Antonio Villanueva in the Jacksonville River Run before succumbing once more to the chronic injuries that have plagued him for most of the past 10 years. Bacheler sees Barry as very much a unique figure in running:

"There are some people who could be tremendous masters competitors if they stay interested in training: Rodgers, Shorter, and Lopes, for example, are all in the 37 year-old range now. But I don't think there are just dozens of Barry Browns around the corner. As hard as he trains and as often as he competes, you'd almost point to him as a great example of how *not* to go about it. Probably for every Barry Brown that makes it there are ten or twenty on the sidelines with chronic injuries from trying to do what he does. I keep thinking it will catch up with him any day now. I'll probably be thinking that when he's winning the 70-and-over division."

Although he graduated with a law degree, Barry has never practiced law. He is self-employed as a life insurance agent who puts together custom designed policies with income tax benefits. He works out of an office in his spacious home in Gainesville half the year, the other half he spends in Glens Falls at a summer home, where he has another set of clients. He was recently married, his second, to Bobbi Thompkins, a vivacious, athletic 29-year-old who is something of a computer whiz. She has managed to program his complex insurance packages so that financial projections can be done quickly. She will also soon make him a father again—he has two daughters by a previous marriage.

If you wonder how someone like Barry Brown manages to squeeze everything into a 24-hour day without going stark raving bonkers, the formula seems to be precisely this: Half of Barry's life revolves around scheduling the other half. He will have extended discussions with training partners to plan out the details of a single workout, he will spend half an hour with a friend working out a way to get in a tennis match the next day, several minutes with Bobbi organizing plans for dinner or an evening out. These sessions all sound alike: We-can-leave-your-car-at-the-track-and-pick-it-up-after-we-get-groceries-and-then-we-can . . . The hours of his day fit together like a Chinese puzzle, with no seams showing once assembled.

"I find that the less you do, the lazier you get. If I try to take a vacation and say I'm going to do nothing but run and lie on the beach, I am more likely to miss a workout than if I'm doing something every minute. I can't stand to be inactive. I hate weekends when I don't have a race. I don't know what to do with myself," he said.

Barry is a far cry from the introspective, lone-wolf long distance runner, and if fact, insists that one of the reasons he has been able to maintain quality training over the years is a steady supply of eager training partners. He well known for his garrulous nature on long runs.

"It's like turning on a tape recorder," said long-time friend League. "All you have to do is get him going on something and you'll never have to say another word. Sometimes when Marty runs with us, they'll start a debate about something or the other and argue their positions passionately for ten miles. The next day, they'll trade sides and do it all over again. We never have a dull run."

Barry, ever the raconteur, truly enjoys training repartee. Liquori figures in his latest favorite anecdote: "Marty and I were jogging in Central Park before the New York marathon last October and we just started running into people. Pretty soon Rodgers and someone else from Boston, then Greg Meyer joined us, and then we ran into John Treacy and another Irish kid from Providence. So Marty says to Treacy, 'Now after your silver medal, how many marathons are you going to run a year?' Treacy says, 'Oh, I'm only going to run one every two years.'

"Marty scoffs at him. 'Come on, you're going to be in big demand. You're not going to turn down all that money.' Treacy says, 'Yes, I am. I'm going to run the European championships, the World Championships, and the Olympics and that's it.' Marty says: 'If someone offers you $80,000 to run a marathon, you're not going to turn that down.' Treacy says, 'Yes I will.' '

"So Marty says 'I'll bet you $5 you run more than one marathon every two years!' And Treacy says, 'Okay, I'll bet!' Then Marty thinks about it a minute and says: 'Naw, it'd be just like an Irishman to turn down $80,000 to win a $5 bet."

Brown doesn't look anywhere near his age, but like most competitive runners, scoffs at the idea that he would run for health or longevity.

"I take those things for granted. When people ask me at clinics, they say, aw you look half your age. You don't look anything near 40, and stuff like that, which is nice. But my father

doesn't look his age either, and he only started running recently. Maybe its genes," he said.

"I still feel like I'm 20 years old, except that something
gone a little wrong. Like there are certain really tough interval
workouts I can't do. Other than that, I don't feel any different
at all. I've given some thought to how long I can keep it up,
but I'm not planning on retiring any time soon. As long as I'm
uninjured and running well, I don't see why I can't continue
into my 50's."

And how do the chronological 20-year-olds feel about
competing head up with geriatric cases?

"Two things. First, I think they respect not only my current
running, but what I've done in the past. At the same time, it
makes them all the more determined not to get beat by a
40-year-old. Some guy who might otherwise ease off a little,
might just put his head down and gut it out when it's a
40-year-old trying to go by him.

It's strange how your perception of these things can
change. I can remember when I was a senior in college, Tom
Laris was coming down to run in an open two-mile I was in. I
can remember thinking to myself, 'I can't let myself get beat by
this old guy.' Well, Laris was running really well that year, even
made the Olympic team. Naturally the 'old guy' just trounced
me.

"He was 29 at the time."

June, 1985

*Current edition note: Tragically, Barry Brown took his
own life on December 14th, 1992. He was said to have had
serious business setbacks and, at a time when he probably
needed running the most, a series of injuries kept him from
training. He was 48 years old.*

Of Myths and Men

A sports-medicine doctor once conducted an informal poll among more than a hundred top runners. The proposition was this: would the athlete take a pill that would allow him to win an Olympic gold medal, but would also cause him to die within a year?

"To my amazement, more than half of the athletes responding stated that they would take my magic pill," he wrote.

Which just goes to show you that there are still some people in sports who have not lost a rather endearing capacity for astonishment.

That study was vaguely reminiscent of a short story Erich Segal wrote some time ago about a frustrated middle-of-the-pack runner who sold his soul to the devil for the ability to run a marathon in two hours flat. It was such a classic insight into the middle-class frustrated jock mentality that I'm sure most of those who read it found the plot line rather uninspired. Who, after all, wouldn't roast in perdition for all eternity for a crack at two flat? A really intriguing scenario would have had some overachieving age-grouper bartering away his immortal essence for a shot at dipping below 2:48.

Sport, in the last quarter of the 20th century, seems to

harbor in its heart, a hard kernel of madness. I think of that every time that perennial lunatic runs out of the stands and onto the football field in the middle of the Super Bowl. Have you ever noticed the way the crowd just mumbles nervously, but doesn't boo the dolt? He represents something they cannot quite bring themselves to disapprove of.

Other examples of sports dementia occur with such frequency that they fade into the hubbub of the sports pages:

• It was reported a year or so ago that some high school football coaches in Georgia practice "red-shirting" players, holding them back a year in school so they can mature and get a little bigger before they play their senior year and move on up to the collegiate ranks. This is high school. Semi-barbaric practices of the pigskin set no longer surprise. Particularly memorable was the anecdote in which the coach threw ice on the ground during a hot workout and made the thirsty players fight each other for it.

• Michael Mewshaw's *Short Circuit*, an expose of the incredibly cynical corruption in professional tennis, seemed to stir only the faintest interest among followers of that sport.

• Sports-page stories about rampant recreational drug use, hormone-based training, and the ghoulish ploy of blood re-infusion are so common as to hardly draw comment.

• Cheating in foot races seems to be the order of the day, and the perpetrators are not just the occasional psychopath like Rosie Ruiz, but now include some fairly accomplished competitors. At the 1984 San Francisco Marathon ($50,000 in prize money), no less than nine of the top 100 finishers were found, on videotape, to have cut the course.

It seems to me that we are reaping approximately what we sowed. Occasionally we stop the revelry long enough to send a look-out up for an overview on "sports and society." When he reports back in shock, we nod gravely and turn back to the party.

The collegiate sports scene didn't change much after an alarming series 15 years ago in Sports Illustrated on the ex-

ploitation of the black athlete. The illiterate former All
American halfback dogging a lawn mower or trucking luggage
has become a set piece of socially conscious sports analysis.

Thus you can expect little reaction to the recent
heart-rending cable TV documentary, "Disposable Heroes,"
which chronicled the sad, winding-down existence of some all
but crippled former football players.

But for a real sense of deja vu, take a look at this conclu-
sion of a Carnegie Foundation report on college athletics: "The
fundamental causes of the defects of American college athletics are two: commercialism, and a negligent attitude toward
the education opportunity for which the college exists. To one,
and generally to both, of these inter-acting causes, every short-
coming of college sport can be traced. Both may be abated,
even if neither, in view of the imperfectability of human nature,
can ever be absolutely abolished." The report was written in
1929.

No, whatever is going on here will not find itself amended
or abated by the recommendation of a committee. It is part of
us.

Cultural historian William Irwin Thompson proposes that
we are a culture bereft of myths, and since myths—being the
detritus of history—tell us in veiled metaphors whence we
came, they also give us an idea of who we are and where we are
going. All of that is lost to technological man, he says, hence
the prevailing existential confusion and angst.

But a society that owes allegiance to neither gods nor
kings will cast about for alternatives. In that way we have come
to dote upon our thespians and our athletes, inundating them
with money and fame, demanding of them the drama and the
clear-cut victories our own ambiguous lives lack.

We ask too much of them.

When this process of mythification turns out the likes of
John McEnroe or his Olympic counterparts, Carl Lewis and
Mary Decker, we reject them as unworthy of our expectations.
And our expectations are complex. Because they must stand in

for immortals, athletes must approximate perfection. But because they are the objects of our own fantasies, they must also be reassuringly normal. When the boys find out that the object of their two-fisted, beer-swilling adoration evinces a proclivity for collecting fine crystal, its going to be head-scratching time at the O.K. Corral.

We are not prepared to understand that our demands are so great that the processes by which our athletes attain perfection also tend to produce some fairly neurotic citizens.

The endurance sports for a long time avoided the kinds of excesses associated with the collegiate rat race and the big money team sports. Besides, the endurance athlete who trains upwards of four to six hours a day, regulates everything about his life with an eye towards athletic perfection, that athlete usually recognizes that he is already in a state approaching religious fervor.

Yet when a society cannot accept that as enough, cannot allow an athlete to be merely great rather than perfect, then he may be pushed over the line. On the other side of the line is the bizarre terrain of modern sport excess: victory through chemistry, tricks with red blood cells, 8-year-old neurotics on the tennis courts or baseball fields.

One sports psychologist says that such attitudes are already having a deleterious effect on children who get into organized sports: "Many kids get sick and tired of the system of rewards and punishments—getting reinforced only for winning, never for trying or having fun—and they drop out because they've never really developed strong feelings of attachment, of commitment, to a sport." This from Robert Singer of Florida State University.

Yet hope springs eternal. There are indications that out of the current interest in endurance sports may come a new athletic sanity, a sense of proportion in an era of extremes.

A friend, an executive for an athletics shoe company, is exposed to many different sports. He told me recently: "I spent some time in an airport waiting for a flight, talking to a very interesting woman in her 50's. She was a medical doctor and a Ph.D., and her specialty was nutrition. She lectures all over the world on the subject. It was only after talking to her for almost two hours that I found out she was a runner, and then it was only because she found out who I work for.

"I get the feeling that there is a change of emphasis going on. People are no longer defining themselves as 'a runner,' or 'a triathlete,' but 'someone who runs' or 'someone who plans on entering the Ironman.'

I would like not to interpret this as a sign that we are abandoning yet another route to secular salvation we have found wanting. I would like to believe that we are regaining some appreciation for the classical Greek ideal of athletics.

But I don't know. We have outgrown our myths. And the gods long ago left Olympus.

June, 1985

A Gathering of Legends

Funny, I don't feel very legendary," said Amby Burfoot. Bill Rodgers laughed. "I know what you mean." We were jogging around the marina at the Harbor Town Inn just north of Oxnard, California, the day before a race featuring Amby, Bill, Frank Shorter, '72 Olympian Jeff Galloway, '76 Olympian Don Kardong, '68 Olympian Tracy Smith, and veteran Gary Tuttle, who lives just a few miles down the road from the race. The race was a 10K, a benefit for the Special Olympics, the theme "Legends of the 70's" having been dreamed up by Boulder running event consultant Rich Castro, who, to my knowledge, does not have a single gold chain around his neck.

At 37, Rodgers should have little to complain about. Only last year he finished an eminently respectable eighth in the US marathon trials in 2:13:30. This year he is turning in sub 29-minute 10K times and doesn't consider himself to be far off his best form.

Amby is a different story. A tall, bearded, wire-rimmed fellow, renowned for his sense of humor and his knowledge of running, he is the East coast editor of Runner's World magazine and a highly regarded writer on the subject, but a bout with pneumonia several years ago scarred his lungs terribly, and he says that he has resigned himself to the fact that his running will be forever limited by it.

But as to his status as a legend, I can only relate that we had heard much of him even in Gainesville, back in the days when Frank Shorter was wondering if he should try a weird event on the roads called a "marathon." Most of us, prescient advisers that we were, counseled against it. Amby had won Boston in 1968, had been a teammate of Bill Rodgers and Jeff Galloway at Wesleyan, and was once only a second off the American marathon record in 2:14:29. He was more or less legendary even before that for certain sartorial habits. A teammate of mine at the University of Florida, a miler named Steve Atkinson, used to tell this story:

"Here I was, a freshman at the NCAA national cross country meet, all these stud runners around. I kept looking around and going 'There's so-and-so over there! And there's so-and-so! I'm going to be dead last in a field of hundreds of guys! I have never been so psyched out of my gourd. I came down to the hotel restaurant before the race and there was this wimpy looking guy in this really grubby, spattered, painter's cap, sitting there having his pre-race toast and tea. It turned out he wore this cap all the time, even in races. I said to myself, 'Well, here's at least one guy I can beat.' It turned out to be Amby Burfoot. He won the race."

Rodgers had to do a TV interview, so we dropped him off at the hotel and picked up Shorter and Castro, who had just checked in and were anxious to get in their post-flight run. Shorter started laughing.

"You know, some things never change. I was sort of surreptitiously eyeing Tracy Smith there in the hotel lobby, saying to myself, 'Boy, does he look fit!'"

"Right. And he was doing the same to you," said Amby.

It was a crystalline day, cool, sunny, with a deep blue sky. We ambled along the sidewalk at the edge of the marina, glancing across a veritable forest of bare masts, and might have been persuaded that every 30-foot sailboat in the world was tied up within our view. Shorter talked about the latest in high tech gimmickry ("You notice how nobody in cycling is talking about drugs anymore? They don't need it! Everything is blood doping now!")

A very pretty girl emerges from a sailboat, steps onto the sidewalk, and, seeing us for the first time, stops and just beams.

"Nice smile," says Castro.

"Running is a demographically acceptable activity in a sailboat marina," says Shorter.

Oxnard, California is one of a peculiar type of American community that gives the impression of having been dreamed up on last Sunday morning by some guy stretching his toes in a hot tub. By late Wednesday afternoon the carpet people were just finishing up, and a couple of guys out back want to know where you want the patio furniture. To get to Oxnard, you fly to Los Angeles and then drive north two hours through a Johnny Carson monologue ("Take the Slauson cut-off, get out, cut off your slauson . . ."). All the walls in Oxnard, which give the appearance of solid masonry, resound hollowly when thumped. This is the kind of Spraykrete-over-chicken-wire architecture that used to come in handy for a set designer in need of, say, a Moorish castle.

This is all to say that Oxnard is not exactly my dream destination, and the idea of writing about a gaggle of former stars getting together to cackle over their beer while reliving old war stories gave me pause. Perhaps my misgivings were related to the fact that I had been a foot soldier in a lot of those wars and just maybe, at age 38, I didn't feel exactly ready for that heavy a dose of nostalgia, if you know what I mean.

I should have spared myself the concern. Twenty, thirty, forty years ago, if you had gotten a group of former champions together a decade after the fact, no matter what their sport, you would undoubtedly have found yourself in a roomful of good-natured, beer-paunched, insurance-selling golfers. You could have counted on hearing a couple of funny stories and several hundred anecdotes amusing only to the participants and then you would have expected that about half past midnight the whole show would have gone pretty maudlin on you.

But these guys, these athletes whose careers extended back into the days when there weren't any decent training shoes, who just caught the front swell of the tidal wave of the fitness movement, these runners (you could tell at a glance even in the hotel lobby) have hardly missed a beat. There they were, surrounded by pretty wives, bouncing babies, and bags of running gear. They were happy to see you, happy to be here, happy period. And they were, to a man, fit.

Jeff Galloway flew in from Lake Tahoe where he had just wrapped up the last of his series of summer camps he holds all around the country. In tow are wife Barbara and one of his two startlingly energetic boy children. He is the founder and head of the Phiddipides athletic store chain, recently authored a book on training, regularly writes a newsletter and numerous magazine articles, and is sorry that his summer schedule has kept him from getting in very good shape. He will finish second in the masters, 18th overall, in 32:03.

Don Kardong popped down from Spokane with wife Bridget and two little girls, one still in swaddling clothes. He was fourth in Montreal in '76, is now active in professional road racing administration, his own store, writing (his book *Thirty Phone Booths to Boston* is a stitch), and running the Lilac Bloomsday run. He is also deplorably out of condition and will finish 13th overall in 31:07.

Tracy Smith lives only a couple of hours away in Bishop, CA, where he works for the department of corrections. He is really more of a legend of the sixties, a greatly feared 10,000 meter track specialist, He has recently turned 40 and is training for masters events with a vengeance. He will finish first in the masters here and 17th overall, in a time of 31:42, which he found "disappointing."

Frank Shorter you know about. What you may not know about are the peculiar patterns his airline-oriented life sometimes takes on. "When I get through here, I go to Sun Valley, Idaho to talk to a group of MD's on vacation up there. But get this. They're all from Oxnard!" Shorter has cut back to running only once a day. He is in the process of a divorce. He has taken up aerobics, weight lifting and some other stuff and for possibly the first time in his life has a chest of his own. Five percent body fat may be a definite possibility in the near future. In the final stretch of this race, Shorter will call out to a young local stud he is closing in on: "Hey, don't let an old cripple beat you!" Later he will want to know "if the kid [who sprinted for his life and thereby saved considerable face] has begun shaving yet." Shorter is also distressed he is not running faster, though he is at long last uninjured and is willing to let things ride for awhile. He will finish sixth overall: 30:18.

Bill Rodgers is the only one who is not out and out depressed by his condition. "Oh, I've been cutting down on my mileage some, like everyone else, and I'm not running as many marathons a year as I used to. But I think I'm in O.K. shape—for this time of year anyway." Despite strong challenges from Tuttle (3rd in 29:38) and a talented Redondo Beach runner named Bob Leetch (2nd in 29:17), Rodgers will pull away in the last mile and win comfortably in 29:03.

Later, back at the hotel, Rodgers lay gratefully on a rub-down table as local sports massage guru Marva Young pounded his slight body into silly putty. He looked over out of the blue and said: "You know, about a year ago I got this foot thing, it hurt like crazy. Then I got this knee thing and this hip thing. I thought I was falling apart!" He put his head down to rest for a moment as Marva started on his quads.

"I went to doctors, physiologists. I mean, they helped, but I was still hurting. Then I went to this friend who sells shoes. He looked in my shoes and said 'You don't have any arches in here!' And I didn't. I didn't have any arches in the shoes." He put his head back down.

"I'm fine now," he sighed.

I thought to myself: This guy doesn't have any concept of aging.

I guess I should have known the event would have been anything but maudlin. I can't recall a single war story. Nobody was cackling into their beer, they were too busy running after errant infants ("Kids add a whole new dimension to training," said Amby) and catching up with each other's latest ventures. But then, these runners are on the cutting edge of something the demographically-aware Mr. Shorter is acutely cognizant of. Not one of the legends considers himself a former athlete. I even heard Shorter unabashedly use the term "citizen-athlete."

Training is something that blends seamlessly into their lifestyles. It shows not only in the fitness of their bodies, but in their demeanor, their sheer exuberance. And it shows in a lot of small ways. The night before the race, Frank hopped off the boat on which we had just taken a lovely sundown tour of the Ventura marina. He was resplendent in a bright white sweatsuit bearing his company's logo.

"Should we change?" he asked. "I could put on my dinner sweats."

Oh, I almost forgot to report that your faithful scribe also toed the starting line with the legends (also with several hundred Oxnardians and Dangermouse, Mickey, Goofy, and a couple of large fuzzy creatures called the Berenstein Bears— remember, this is California).

Somewhere around the second mile I dropped Amby and spent at least several seconds feeling sorry about the debilitating condition of his lungs before setting out to get as good a time as I could muster. I was determined to do well in my self-designated "Footnotes of the 70's" division. I soon found out that running a race in Oxnard is something like running a race in Florida, only flatter. I think there was one turn in 6.2 miles and the only hills were speed bumps. As I wheezed into the final straightaway I heard a familiar legendary voice call from behind: "I'm coming, Parker, do you still have a kick?"

It was, of course, the nearly bed-ridden Amby Burfoot, whose lungs had somehow held up long enough to put him within striking distance with 100 yards to go.

"Would you like to tie, or don't you do that sort of thing?" he asked politely.

We tied for 43rd in 34:31, which is disappointing except that neither of us ran a very good race and we aren't in very good shape anyway, although we will be by next year.

December, 1985

Sawdust Memories

The time you won your town the race
We chaired you through the market-place
Man and boy stood cheering by
And home we brought you shoulder-high.

To-day, the road all runners come
Shoulder-high we bring you home,
And set you at your threshold down,
Townsman of a stiller town . . .

Now you will not swell the rout
Of lads that wore their honors out
Runners whom renown outran
And the name died before the man . . .

—*A.E. Housman*
"To An Athlete Dying Young"

It is a sound that defies description," said my friend, "Seventy thousand people roaring. It goes right through you. When you realize that roar is for something you just did, it is an incredible feeling."

He always gives me this little quizzical look when he talks of such things, a smile and a puzzled tilt of the head, not without his normal good humor, asking if I might have an explanation for this sound that will not leave his head.

It is a sound he heard many times at one point in his life, and its echoes will be with him until he dies. He is not, you must understand, a case of a former great athlete who lives in the past, finding solace there from a failed or meaningless present. He is in fact an extremely successful attorney, a contented husband and father, a valued friend to many. He rarely talks about sports, and then only when someone else brings the subject up. I suspect he never says anything about the roar in his head to anyone except his wife or to friends he knows will "understand."

There was a time, you see, when he could move down the autumn sidelines like a chill wind, and take a pass high over his shoulder in a precise and graceful arc. Leaping, one-handed, over, under and between defenders, he gathered in the irascible object whenever it was humanly possible and often when it was not. So terrible and beautiful was his art that some were occasionally embarrassed and surprised to find—amidst the shrieks and tumult of pompoms—tears in their eyes.

At the end of his sophomore season, in the autumn of his 20th year, they made him an All-American. Then all he had to do was live with it for the next half century.

I am not quite sure why early success in athletics should cast such a haunting shadow over the later lives of athletes, but there seems to be no question that it does. And the success need not be on an Olympic scale, either. A couple of good J.V. games in high school is probably enough. Perhaps even, as in Irwin Shaw's short story, The Eighty-Yard Run, a really good practice may leave one marked for life.

A most succinct expression of that shadow can be found in Fred Exley's A Fan's Notes, in which he reminisces about his father, a well-known local athlete in Watertown, NY in the

30's. After high school the elder Exley had been courted by several colleges, but had given up football to marry and start a family: "My father became an unhappy lineman—he loathed that job to desperation!—for the Niagara Mohawk, struggled to eke out a subsistence for his wife and children, and took his pleasure in the grim Sunday afternoon world of semi-professional athletes seeking violently to recapture a sense of a talent that may never have existed."

From a perspective of long years, Exley concluded: "Now I can also understand that my father, for all his melancholy aspect, was as happy as any man can be who has performed his most poetic feats before twenty."

Housman's solution for the roar in the head of the ex-hero is simply to die before it gets to be much of a problem. It is a neat resolution, preserving one's fame intact while at the same time avoiding embarrassing the rest of us by hanging around, a constant reminder that, as Proust suggested, those little things whizzing by our ears like bees are, in fact, minutes.

When I was younger, I used to find myself referring to retired heroes in the past tense ("Peter Snell didn't have the build of a miler . . ."), as if they had died already. It occurred to me as something of a revelation one day that Peter Snell was in fact very much alive. Imagine how those athletes feel when someone does that to their face: "You sure had a great kick, Mr. Snell."

Most athletes do not die young, however, and people seem to be fascinated by what happens to them. For that reason I keep a special file marked "The Aging Athlete," from which emanates a palpable nostalgia.

Here is an article from it, for instance, about Ingemar Johansson, who beat Floyd Patterson to become heavyweight champion of the world in 1959. Later, Patterson knocked him out twice, and Johansson went from being a household word to virtual obscurity in less than a year. He handles the roar in his head in a unique way:

"In my life I like to move around," he said. "Three, four,

five years in one place and then move to the next place. It's a good way to live, You can choose exactly the kind of weather you want." The writer, Bob Greene, had found him running a small motel in Pompano Beach. Johansson liked the relative anonymity of living in the United States as opposed to his native Sweden. "I can't even explain to you what it is like to be Ingemar Johansson in Sweden," said his son. "The night my father won the championship is the only thing in peoples lives that they remember exactly where they were. It is like when President Kennedy died in America."

There is a piece in my file about Mickey Mantle, written by Peter Gent, an ex-footballer who understands the roar about as well as anyone: 'I work for this chemical company,' Mickey says, 'I go to their sales meetings and golf outings—they call it motivational or something. I get a lot of requests for personal appearances . . . Don't get me wrong, I'm glad to be getting the work . . . but it sure is a lot of traveling, and—' he gropes for the words—'It's just sort of . . . strange. On the street in New York, people still come up and throw their arms around me and start crying . . . .'

And then there is Mantle's recurrent dream: "I'm in a taxi, trying to get to Yankee Stadium. I'm late, and I've got my uniform on. But when I get there, the guard won't let me in. He doesn't recognize me. So I find this hole in the fence, and I'm trying to crawl through it, you know? But I can only get my head in. I can see Billy and Whitey and Yogi and Casey. And I can hear the announcer: 'Now batting . . . number seven . . . Mickey Mantle.' But I can't get through the hole. That's when I wake up. My palms are all sweaty."

We all, I suspect, have our own versions of that dream.

And how is Mantle making it these days? Gent writes: "Well, he can't practice his art anymore, and he misses his friends. They were good company. They weren't car dealers or insurance swindlers or killers or land developers. And most of all, they weren't trying to devour him, dead or alive. They were the players acting out one of the great dramatic rituals of the

1950's and 60's: the pennant races of the New York Yankees. Yes, hitting a home run in Yankee Stadium to win a game for teammates he regarded as fellow travelers in a world that was mad outside the white lines was a high that Mantle will never recapture. He still dreams about being locked out of Yankee Stadium or about making comebacks that end in brutal humiliation and failure. It is Mickey's tiger, and he struggles with it constantly. It is a son of a bitch."

To qualify for my file, the athlete need not have been a gold medalist or champion of the world. On the contrary, one prized clipping is a local newspaper story about Rey Robinson, a Florida A & M sprinter who is best-known for a race he didn't run. Because of a coach's incredibly inane screw-up, Robinson and teammate Eddie Hart didn't get to the stadium in time to run their semi-finals in the 1972 Olympic 100 in Munich.

I met Rey one day on the A & M campus recently. I was at the football field, chatting with another former A & M sprinter of some note, Bob Hayes, when Rey, now a sprint coach at the school, sauntered up and greeted him. Hayes introduced Rey as "the guy who missed the race," which, after 12 years, Rey seemed entirely used to. They talked for awhile and then a sort of strange well-haven't-you-figured-out-what-to-do-either? Uneasiness set in. Hayes has had his own problems over the years, but at least he got his gold medal—two, in fact. And then many good years of pro football. He made a lot of money and he spent a lot of money and the last I heard, he was driving a truck for a living. The thing is, the uneasiness was the same for both of them, the golden boy and the guy who missed the bus. I expect that Mary Decker will be in my file one day, and that hers will be a sad story, too.

The latest addition to my file is the recounting, by Gary Smith in Sports Illustrated, of an Ali/Foreman meeting 10 years after their titanic battle in Zaire: "At last Ali appeared, taking small, slow steps like sips from a drink he no longer wanted. He wore slacks and a sport shirt and carried his shoes. His eyes seemed glazed, almost as if he were in a trance, but they flickered when he saw Foreman, and the two men embraced. Ali lowered himself slowly onto a sofa and said, 'I'm getting old.'

The two fighters, rounded and softened by the years, regard each other with something like love. They talk religion. Ali prays five times a day and Foreman is minister of a tiny church outside Houston. Each worries that the other is on the Wrong Path. They try to convert each other. Ten years after they faced each other in that ring in Zaire, the most dangerous unarmed men in the world, Foreman worries that an aimless Ali will commit suicide.

I wonder if either realizes that what he is really doing is wrestling with his own tiger, dealing in some way with the roar that will never leave his head?

In many of these stories is a common fixation: the ex-champ sweeping up. Literally. In the Foreman/Ali piece, there is a photograph of Foreman worrying the linoleum in his church with a broom, with the caption: "Foreman doesn't mind that his church is small and attendance sparse and that he is also the custodian."

Greene begins the Johansson story: "The last white heavyweight boxing champion of the world finished making his final bed of the morning. He swept up in front of the motel, then waited to see if any more guests would be checking in."

And Gent, talking with Mantle about ex-athletes' drinking problems, wrote: "I mention an ex-pro football player who actually has given up drinking. Mantle doesn't seem to hear, but I continue anyway. Now this guy spends a lot of time walking around picking up little pieces of trash in the parking lot of his motel. I think it helps him."

I'm not quite sure what attracts writers to such images, but I confess that I'm not immune. Somewhere in my photo files are some pictures I once took of Frank Shorter mowing his lawn and peeling some carrots.

It is nearly a cliché that attitudes about sports are changing rapidly. There is less emphasis on those games that require the lightning reflexes of youth and more on those requiring stamina and experience. There is more doing and less watching. Champions like Carlos Lopes push back long-assumed age barriers.

A little appreciated but eminently humane benefit of these changes—at least to those of us who seemed to grow up in locker rooms of one kind or another—will be to take some of the melancholy out of the change in seasons, to make less distinct and harsh that line between athlete and ex-athlete.

Perhaps that means that I will one day have no need for my file, because there will be no morbid fascination with the lives of ex-champions. It is only a fascination based, after all, on the unconscious knowledge that the athlete faces his own mortality earlier than everyone else.

As to those ex-champions, whether they be sweeping up or filing appellate briefs, I doubt that anyone should waste much sympathy on them. Perhaps the only thing worse than dealing with the roar of the crowd in your head is never having heard it in the first place.

January 1985

The Howard Cosell Syndrome

I don't miss Howard Cosell much. Oh, his grating nasal voice and his infuriatingly pedantic manner didn't bother me nearly so much as the feeling that he and I were always witnessing entirely different events.

That my perception of a sporting event doesn't match someone else's shouldn't be surprising. Though I have long been fascinated by, and long written about athletics, I have always suspected that my interest was of a different variety than that of, say, the newspaper sports writer, whose primary concerns are: Who won? How did they do it? and (more and more, it seems) How much are they getting paid for it?

I am not particularly proud of this aberration. In fact I make this public confessional somewhat sheepishly. It took a long time to figure out why I rarely have the answers to the very basic questions of friends who have just entered the room in the middle of a football game as I sit, apparently enraptured. Who's got the ball? What's the score? And even: Who's playing? The word is out: Don't bother to ask Parker, the proverbial guy who Doesn't Know the Score.

Yet there it is. I am only remotely interested in the score, and even then the interest is removed, abstract. The score is of import only insofar as it affects the strategy of the moment: An algorithm of cold numbers insufficiently subtle to convey the contained, dangerous, beautifully complex warfare that is American football. Or championship tennis. Or pro basketball. Or a world-class marathon for that matter.

This is not another one of those anti-competition diatribes by some zoned-out ethereal type who believes we can get all the athletics we need by zinging Frisbees on the commons. I'm not even hinting that winning isn't important. Hell, it's the heart and soul of what is going on out there. But the guys or gals out on the field are paying more than enough attention to that little detail, and in the final analysis, we all win and we all lose anyway. I'd rather focus on the poetry.

What my perspective really boils down to is that rather than rooting for one side or another, in effect identifying with one team's (or individual's) fans and supporters, I find myself identifying in a rather general way with the athletes of both sides. When watching football, I particularly focus on the quarterback and the receivers; I suppose because to an old basketball player their maneuvers are more familiar than those of the linemen and running backs. My allegiance, if any, is likely to shift several times during a contest, and is usually pledged to the underdog. Nothing is more satisfying than a hard and well fought contest that finds the underdog tying the score at the end and forcing an overtime. The final outcome then seems almost beside the point. What catharsis! What joy! We don't have to stop playing yet!

I feel great empathy and sympathy—when his own fans often do not—for the athlete who attempts with grace something difficult and fails. Geoff Smith's gallant effort in the face of impossible conditions at Boston a few years back comes to mind, as does Frank Shorter's loss to Cierpinski in the rain at Montreal, and Jim Ryun's hopeless attempt to run down mountain-trained Kipchoge Keino in the thin air of the Mexico City Olympics. What a sad loss, the spectator unable to be ennobled by noble failure.

My blood used to boil when Cosell would condemn a quarterback who—under pressure, running left and throwing right—underthrew his receiver by a foot and was thus intercepted. Most athletes know all too well that running left and throwing right is a maneuver biomechanically at odds with itself, forcing a player to deal with the Newtonian problem caused by the opposite directions of his body and the ball. He does so with a sheer preponderance of arm strength and an unfathomable skill. Its counterpart in basketball is the fade-away jump shot, in which a player—leaping upwards and backwards away from the hoop—pays for a few inches of free space from his opponent with the same kind of barely comprehensible skill. These types of maneuvers, which great athletes perform with enough regularity to make them look easy, increase geometrically the difficulty of the ordinary forward pass, the ordinary jump shot, the ordinary anything. Yet I dare say that the great majority of spectators, often including our "expert commentators" and occasionally even highly-regarded coaches, are insensitive to many of the acts of physical poetry they are privileged to witness.

I saw a clear example of this myopia in this year's NCAA semi-final game between St. Johns and Georgetown. Chris Mullins, a wonderfully skillful 6-6 St. Johns guard drove past his opponent and suddenly found himself one-on-one with a 7-foot Georgetown tree named Patrick Ewing. Ewing wanted Mullins badly, you could see it is his eyes. He skyed up so high his outstretched hand must have been two feet above the rim, ready to deliver Mullins the dreaded leather sandwich.

Mullins was already in the air and none of his teammates was open, so he did something at once so poetic and so subtle that if you understood it and if you love basketball as I do, it would surely have brought a little catch to your throat. Instead of driving all the way to the hoop and hoping for a miracle or a foul, Mullins brought his drive up a little short, rotated slightly away from Ewing (all this in mid-air mind you) and lofted an incredibly beautiful, soft, underhand lay-up with an arch on it so high that it was almost a parody, so high that it glanced off the very upper left hand corner of the backboard as it came down. Ewing swatted at the ball furiously, but it eluded him by a few incredibly frustrating millimeters. It was the kind of shot you might practice for years and use two or three times in a career.

Well, Mullins did not make the shot, but he came so close I was already out of my seat ready to scream praises to the TV screen. The ball bobbled in the rim and hopped out. But it was the skill and daring of the very attempt that was so thrilling. Finding himself at a complete physical disadvantage, this great athlete nonetheless turned imminent humiliation into near triumph with a split second of sheer grace and skill. But what did the "expert commentator" talk about? He talked about how high Patrick Ewing had jumped.

Patrick Ewing is of course a great athlete himself. But in that one confrontation, he had merely exhibited his admittedly awesome physical prowess and timing. What Mullins had produced was something approaching art. Yet it went unremarked upon.

What I'm saying, I suppose, is that people like Howard Cosell who have never tried to run left and throw right in their lives should probably not be eligible to critique those who have. In Cosell's case, fortunately, during much of his broadcasting career he was bracketed by former exceptional athletes who would occasionally, and very gently, attempt to provide insight more informed by experience. Perhaps to some viewers it seemed they were just trying to soft-pedal the boneheaded mistakes of their fellow jocks, I don't know. But I can't ever recall Gifford or Meredith or Karras saying anything about some physical maneuver performed by a player that struck me as clearly off-the-wall or wrong-headed as many of Cosell's observations.

One exchange between Cosell and Dandy Don Meredith comes to mind. Paraphrasing as best I can recall it, it went something like this:

COSELL: I CAN'T understand how a RECEIVER could MISS a catch like that.

MEREDITH: Well, Howard, I think you ought to go a little easier on old Fred. The way the wind held the ball up, he had to switch over and try to take it over his left shoulder at the last second. Going full tilt like that, it's a mighty tough adjustment to make . . .

GIFFORD: I think Don makes a good point there, Howard.

COSELL: My opinion is STILL that a PROFESSIONAL athlete, getting paid the SALARY he gets paid to catch footballs, SHOULD have CAUGHT THAT PASS.

There was just a brief moment of what I took to be pretty tense silence, followed by Meredith's sardonic capper: "Yeah, but what do you know?"

It was a very good question.

September, 1985

Still Shorter

Over the years I had heard stories about the "aloof" Frank Shorter, a cool, detached businessman who never seemed to loosen up properly at the party. He would impulsively cancel or ignore a commitment, I was told. He would fail to kiss the baby or would refuse to wear the funny hat. He was somehow smaller or skinnier or less entertaining than he was on TV.

Which was all very strange to hear. I usually responded to these stories by recalling a time when Frank's biggest problem in the whole world was my exhaust pipe.

On hot spring nights in Gainesville, after 20-mile days, Frank and I would get on my 125 CC motorcycle and buzz down to a little place inappropriately called "The Gay 90's," there to drink surprising amounts of beer. Frank complained that my rakishly-angled motorcross exhaust pipe, which ended right behind his back pocket, was always filling his jacket with carbon monoxide and was probably even as we spoke poisoning his system. They had wonderful popcorn at the Gay 90's, and gumball-type machines with pistachios, and foosball tables. Frank was the best sort of Friend-of-Your-Youth companion to have: intelligent, witty, introspective (but Kenny Moore came up with the best adjective for Frank: sweet). We still thought of the Olympics as some kind of noble and magical athletic rite, a single apolitical constant in a changing and strife-ridden world. Our favorite movie was M*A*S*H, which we thought a wonderful paradigm for life, and our plans were rather vaguely to run in the Olympics and then open up a law practice somewhere. Some of my happiest moments on earth were spent in that place with Frank discussing the exhaust pipe problem and just exactly how profound Kurt Vonnegut really was. It was, as I say, a simpler time.

Whenever I catch up with Frank nowadays, I always experience that peculiar falling-horizontally sensation you feel when you step onto the moving sidewalk at the airport. You can see it coming but somehow it doesn't help.

"Ah, you're here," Frank said on the phone. I was in Boulder, stupid from jet lag. "Okay, here's the plan . . ." I had purposely tried to come during the middle of a slow week but it seemed that Louise, Frank's wife of 13 years, was up at their recently purchase house in Vail, trying to get it ready for the skiing season, so Frank had the two boys, Alex, 5, and Markey, 2. Also, Frank's brother Same was in town, having just finished up an extremely drawn-out divorce that very afternoon. Also, we were going out to eat at Chucky Cheese, which is a sort of miniature Disneyland with pizza. It is at Chucky Cheese where they put some kind of secret compound in the food that doesn't affect adults but turns kids into miniature lunatics.

Here is how it goes.

"Markey, no skee-ball until you finish your pizza." says Dad Frank.

And Markey, a grinning little blue-eyed devil, sort of gums a piece of crust and then disappears into the game room with a handful of brass Chucky Cheese tokens. He and Alex reappear at regular intervals to be bought off again and again while Frank, Sam, and I rather dourly assess the state of mankind and so on.

Frank talked about the truly tumultuous time he has had with his sportswear business, which has included several changes of partners, a few takeover attempts, and the assorted selection of rabbit punches and cheap shots that give a certain stratum of American business its wonderful aroma.

"Hey, lissen," he says, doing an excellent Jewish trader, "So you say you wanna get in the garment biznizz?" There is the same sly humor of old, but there is also some genuine pain in his voice.

Clearly both his and Louise's lives have been complicated enormously by Frank Shorter Sportswear, Inc. as well as by his small chain of retail stores. But to show how easy it is to lose the recent historical perspective, I asked him why he had gotten so heavily involved in the businesses himself rather than merely striking a licensing agreement with another company.

He had to remind me that such arrangements were simply taboo when he started out. I had all but forgotten about the time when you couldn't even hold a legitimate coaching job and still maintain your amateur status. If the top running stars are able to make relatively uncomplicated livings for themselves these days, it is in large part because Frank and a handful of others cleared a lot of brush a few years back.

He has tried to act as if it was all perfectly normal for a runner in serious training to also attempt to monitor a multi-million dollar business, but he was always straining mightily to fit everything in. In many ways, he was a victim of his own success. "At the end of the first month we were $6 million back-ordered," he said grimly.

The next day, as we were leaving the busy hive of his sportswear warehouse, out of the blue he responded to a question I had not even asked: "You see? There will be plenty for me to do when I don't run any more."

He was clearly protesting too much, and I was not surprised when he recently concluded the sale of the company to Levi Straus on very happy terms, achieving one long-term goal

far more important than finding something to occupy his time
after running: simplifying his life.

Despite Frank's enormous athletic success in Munich and
afterwards, nothing seemed to have worked out for him in real
life the way we had supposed in our Gay 90's daydreams. That
is something else I have to keep reminding myself about Frank's
success: that it was accomplished in a crucible of turmoil, strife,
and outright violence. After the slaughtered Israeli athletes at
Munich, surely no athlete could ever come back to the
Olympic Games with quite the same innocence, particularly an
athlete as sensitive and perceptive as Frank Shorter.

Then there was the tragic death of his good friend Steve
Prefontaine in a car crash in 1975, and soon thereafter Frank's
emotional Congressional testimony concerning pay-offs in
amateur athletics, an act of defiance and honesty that might
have destroyed his athletic career right then without some
quick legal footwork. The guardians of hypocrisy in the AAU
weren't much on sleuthing, but they would always accept a live
sacrifice.

This was also the era in which we first heard the ghoulish
rumors about folks trying to pump themselves with an extra
quart of their own blood for a race. This was the beauty of
sport that moved Pindar to verse? What had happened to our
innocent dreams of running foot-races free in the sunshine?

What were we to tell the kiddies?

In America in the last quarter of the 20th century we have
few unretouched heroes who don't sooner or later jump into a
fountain or set themselves on fire or otherwise demand guarded reassessment. Such behavior is supposedly a function,
depending upon your point of view, of the pervasiveness of the
media, the stress of life at the top, the potency of the drugs,
and so on.

Whatever, we expect a great deal of those heroes; more
than they ever offered, more than most of them could reason-

ably be expected to give. Even after Frank had won the gold medal in the 1972 Olympics, high school guys were writing him for training schedules, and he was sending them, written out by hand.

That sort of thing could not go on, of course, but there wasn't anyone around at the time to explain how you are supposed to go about organizing yourself as an American institution. Frank was thus thrust out into the new and used hero market to fend for himself. For someone as sensitive, intelligent, and introspective as Frank, it must have been a truly unsettling experience.

It is one of the singular hallmarks of fame in this country if you are famous, somebody somewhere will give you $5,000 just to get on a plane and come on over.

The price varies surprisingly little (ex-presidents get a bit more, former astronauts and place kickers from Super Bowl teams get a bit less). You will be expected to say a few words or perhaps show an inspirational film. That part of it hardly matters. You are really there so they can see what you look like.

The dynamics of this peculiar reality began to have more than a little to do with shaping Frank Shorter's life after Munich. Frank admits to having a hard time saying no. Which is just fine with a lot of the kind of people he has had to deal with because they don't take no for an answer anyway.

And there were of course opportunities that could scarcely be passed up: "I turn down a lot of endorsements because it just wouldn't be honest. But when you get paid obscene amounts of money to say you like something you really do like . . ." Thus he has occasionally done things like fly to Chicago at three a.m. to film a United commercial because that was the only time they could get hold of a 747 to use as a prop.

His track and field commentary has always been colorful, perceptive, and clearly reflective of much background work, whether he opined on the marathon or the high jump. "I' Always like the commentary work because I am a real track and field fan. I've watched some of the other stars who go into announcing and it's obvious that they never really paid any attention to any other events than their own." That would not be Frank, who used to lay around the dorm room, devouring every issue of Track and Field News, cover to cover. A week later he would make a remark about somebody who was ranked third in the hammer on the US lists. So add to the agenda yet another career many would find challenging in and of itself.

"At times the pressures built up until he simply couldn't handle it and he would blow up," said Louise, the usual recipient of such blow-ups. However well he seemed to manage, Frank really does not have the disposition for the kind of lifestyle that has been thrust upon him. He is at heart a quiet, contemplative, and decent fellow who believed most everything they told him at Yale about the brotherhood of man.

His response over the years to the pressures and to the rough and tumble of the business world has been to circle the wagons closer and closer. When I was out to visit in 1976, shortly before the Montreal Olympics, there was a steady little group of runners training with him. They would be sitting politely in the front yard of his house at the foot of Flagstaff Mountain twice a day when he emerged to run.

"Who do you train with in Boulder these days?" I asked. We were in Tulsa last fall, jogging the day before a race.

"No one," he said.

We ran on in silence for awhile. I asked him if he didn't miss the camaraderie of the old Gainesville bunch. He didn't reply. Maybe he didn't hear me.

"I was extremely lucky. First of all, my foot was broken. For all practical purposes I was limping," Frank said of his silver medal in Montreal. We were chatting in the lobby of a Tulsa hotel before he went up to give an inspirational talk to a group of Xerox executives. "Secondly, you have to remember that 30 seconds behind were two others people. Thirty seconds in a marathon is from here to across the street. That is something not many people realized. I was very lucky."

He was quiet for awhile, re-living it a little, one more time, as athletes are doomed to do. There he said wistfully:

"I keep wondering, hell, what kind of shape must I have been in if I could run that fast limping? Maybe that's the frustration, the challenge to try to regain that without the impediment . . ." He seems almost in a trance. Then he shakes his head as if to clear it: "I don't know, maybe I'm too old. Mimoun did it in '56 when he was 37, but . . ."

The next day he runs the 15K Tulsa Run in around 47:30, which he feels is satisfactory for his recent training. He made a quip to the crowd about hanging around for the age-group listings like everyone else.

Frank has been so visible that it is difficult to keep in mind that he has been more or less continuously injured for most of the past six years. He would on occasion be able to train consistently enough to run a good race or two, even surprising the likes of Rod Dixon once or twice. But his training was erratic at best. At a time when he perhaps most needed it, he was denied the one comfort he had always counted on: his prowess in racing flats. He has spent—and still spends—a great deal of time on the stationary bike, trying desperately to finesse the thing.

"I couldn't maintain it," he said. "My form was off, I would be running to compensate and I would get all tied up. Then I'd get another injury." He says it with the kind of resignation that only one who has truly been through that particular wringer can say it. It is beyond irony and beyond weariness.

"Remember how we used to have a good day and sort of take it for granted? Well, one of the big differences in training is now when I have a good day, I really cherish it . . ." he said.

In America in the last quarter of the 20th century we have few unretouched heroes who don't sooner or later jump into the hotel fountain or set themselves on fire or otherwise demand guarded reassessment. Such behavior is supposedly a function, depending upon your point of view, of the pervasiveness of the media, the stress of life at the top, the potency of the drugs, and so on.

We expect a great deal of our heroes; more than they ever really offered, more than most of them could reasonably be expected to give. Even after Frank had won the gold medal, high school guys were writing him for training schedules, and he was sending them, written out by hand.

He kept that sort of thing up for as long as he could. I watched him trying.

At this writing, his training continues to go well. He is running in excess of 100 miles a week, at altitude, intervals included. He is serious about making the Olympic team.

He runs, as he has for some time now, alone.

April, 1984

Frank didn't make the qualifying time for the 1984 trials. He petitioned to be allowed to run anyway, but was turned down. Now a masters runner, he stays close to 30-minute 10K shape. He has divorced and remarried, and still lives in Boulder. (1988)

Current edition note: Shorter to this day keeps up a remarkable schedule. He has become an accomplished masters cyclist and biathlete, still does a great deal of television commentary and speaking.

Watch out for the Women

"It is precisely the female athletes who, being positively interested in their own game, feel themselves least handicapped in comparison to the male ... "

—Simone De Beauvoir, *The Second Sex*

Oh, hey, I may be slow, but I eventually catch on all right all right. You've got to remember I come from a different era. Ten years ago there was a girl named Bobby who ran the three-mile warm-up course every day with some of the Florida Track Club guys and we all thought she was really something; an appealing oddity, like a one-legged tap dancer.

Then there was Peachtree in '78, I finished disgusted, somewhere in the 60's, with a time in the low 33's, my slowest time for several months. But I can still remember the special little tingle of fear I felt when I learned that Mary Decker had finished not very far behind. Coming from a track background, I used to joke with fellow milers that a sure sign of degenerating ability was being passed in a "road race" (it was a pejorative term) by someone wearing a funny hat. Now, only a few years into the running boom, here was a new—and very real—challenge.

A few summers ago Julie Shea, at running camp in the mountains in North Carolina, wanted me to do 220's with her on the track. She was tuning up for the Maggie Valley 5-miler. I had talked to Jack Bacheler, her coach, only a few days earlier and he had warned me (with an ironic chuckle that indicated maybe *he* couldn't quite believe it either): "Hey, listen, watch out for her. If you're not ready, she'll run you into the ground."

"Sure you don't want to run just a few of them, easy pace?" Julie asked after I had already demurred once.

"Hell no," I told her.

"Don't cuss at me," said the strictly raised Ms. Shea.

There was no getting around it. My legs were sore from the hill running, I was generally not in very good shape, and it dawned on me with unmerciful clarity that I didn't want to run those 220's with Julie because I *really couldn't keep up.* My attitude, though, had changed considerably since Peachtree in '78. Simply put, I had a great deal of respect for Julie as an athlete; after all she had just finished running a marathon in 2:30:3 (3rd at Boston in '81), three minutes faster than my best (and only) marathon time. If there is one thing runners come to grips with sooner or later, it is the grim egalitarianism of the stopwatch. I didn't want to run those 220's because I realized that *as an athlete* I simply wasn't on her level at the time.

Then, finally, there was last summer, same camp: Roy Benson's Florida Distance Runners' Camp in Brevard, NC

Group 1 was our version of the "A Team," the burners. Tom Raynor, a Nike rep and a 31:00 10K runner, and I were voted "most likely to keep up" by Benson and his staff, and thus we were put in charge of these fire-breathers. The A Team boasted the likes of University of Florida's Keith Brantly (28:07), several other college and high school champions, and two or three extremely over-achieving masters runners. Quarter was neither asked nor taken. Blitzing along at 6:30

pace at a place called Cat Gap one day, someone took a wrong turn and a planned "7-mile" run came in at just under 15. Dinner was almost missed and the Division of Forestry had been put on stand-by alert, but not a whimper was heard from the A Team. The next day there were cautionary but light-hearted warnings about taking (this with an eerie sci-fi lilt to the voice) "the trail that time forgot . . . "

But for Raynor and I the truly unusual thing about our bunch (we would look back and forth in something close to awe during runs) was the female contingent. At various times during the two weeks, it consisted of: Ann Audain, Katy Shilley, Linda McLennan, and the aforementioned Julie Shea. These were killer trails we were running, often twice a day, occasionally so steep as to be literally hand over hand, with occasional slimy-log-over-rocky-creek crossings (broken bones here a genuine possibility). Competition being what it generally is at camp (what it is, is *fierce*), most afternoon "workouts" tended to become semi-races, and Raynor and I watched the women in wonderment. They were, well, *undaunted.*

"That Ann Audain!" I would say.

"Ain't it great?" said Raynor.

"She's a trooper!"

"Yeah boy!"

Among the other runners we noticed an interesting phenomenon. At the slimy log crossings and other tricky places, the masters tended to pay a little extra attention to the women; nothing very overt, just a glance back or a friendly word. But the younger guys, who have probably grown up racing against—and possibly getting beaten by—female runners, gave them not a second thought. It was Katie-bar-the-door, devil-take-the-hindmost, and blast on down that trail that time forgot . . .

You cannot politic your way around the black and white reality of a runner's ability (or lack thereof). There is no way to "fake it 'til you make it," no "helpful" image to project, no way to dress for success.

Group 1 was composed solely of talented, capable, tough-minded athletes. That was what struck Tom Raynor and I. Those women unarguably *belonged* there.

It was a delightful thing to behold.

That bellwether of urban corporate club jocks everywhere, *Esquire* magazine, recently published a piece called "Men Competing With Women" (May, 1983). Naturally the focus was on that one he-man sport that is most clearly taking the country by storm: squash. The import of the piece was that women have now progressed athletically to the point that a woman's national champion can be expected to give a good account of herself against a male club "A" player and how are we going to take that, fellas?

Running, writer Frank Satterthwaite discerned, seemed a bit ahead of the times:

"In situations in which women have proven themselves in co-ed competition, the emphasis has shifted from threat to challenge. Paul Glum, an excellent club runner who heads a runners club for the West Side YMCA in New York, told me about a recent 10K race he'd run. For most of the race he was running neck and neck with a blonde who was the lead woman. But then suddenly, toward the end, along came this black-haired woman. She passed him. He pulled away from the blonde but couldn't catch the black-haired woman.

'I tried to kick at the end, but she had too much distance,' he recalled. 'I'll look for her in future races. I'd like to beat her.'

Why? Because she's a woman?

'No, because it's a standard I can relate to. I could never challenge the top male runners. Being a man, maybe I want to be able to run like Alberto Salazar, but it's not going to happen. If I can keep up with the top woman, though, that's an achievement. Something I can go for.' Which explains the pleasure [a club squash pro] took in beating [a woman national squash champion]. She represented attainable excellence."

Which is one way, I suppose, of looking at things. I don't know Paul Glum, nor how excellent a runner he is, but if he or the majority of other male runners out there think that Joan Benoit and some of her colleagues represent some kind of "attainable excellence," they all need to do some serious re-evaluating. With her devastating 2:22 Boston time, Ms. Benoit has just given most of us a healthy taste of quite *unattainable* excellence.

Road racing is the one sport in which men and women compete head up in the same competition. There is theoretically no contact, and no ball to take funny bounces. It is perhaps the perfect arena in which the two sexes can thrash out, in good humor (good sportswomanship?) and all that, once and for all, the various slings and arrows of several million years of evolution.

And unlike other sports, women have been involved in competitive road racing since the beginning, growing with the sport. For that reason perhaps our sport provides the discerning observer with a window into the future, a glimpse of what a more sexually egalitarian society will be like.

March, 1984

All in the Family

The helicopter shuttle sets down at the outskirts of what author Benjamin Stein calls "the derationalized zone" (better known as Los Angeles). Though it is past midnight, the hot breath of the Santa Anna blows over the Saddleback Mountains and gives the skin on your face the general texture of the kind of lake bed where they land space shuttles.

This is El Toro, CA, where I have been sent to examine a somewhat predictable phenomenon of the growing but still small subculture of world class runners: a guy and gal who are at the same time certifiably elite and legally married. I am trying hard not to act like a reporter from *People* magazine.

"I hope this doesn't mess up your article," says Tom Wysocki, throwing my bags in the back of his Mazda RX-7, "but I just quit my job at Tiger." Since he doesn't seem like a man unduly burdened by the rigors of unemployment, and since wife Ruth, who is usually up before dawn for her morning five, has long since turned in, I suggest we search Orange County for a six-pack and talk it over.

It turns out that Tom Wysocki, 27, is not unemployed at all, but has merely switched to Brooks, a move that will give him more time to train seriously for a shot at the US team, and will mercifully remove him from his daily wrestling matches with the vagaries of the Japanese approach to business.

"It finally got to the point that no matter how much I agreed with my supervisor, I was still wrong. It was not a good situation," he sighed. He sips a can of Olympia.

It is hardly surprising Wysocki didn't particularly fit in with the Osaka-headquartered Tiger company. Obsessive-compulsive he is not. His style is, in fact, modified west coast. Good-natured, intelligent, somewhat bemused: a sort of (if you'll bear with me) likable, non-obnoxious, blond version of Sonny Bono.

And Ruth, 26, who stands just a shade taller than her 5-7 husband, is so affable as to make you wonder if she is not rather sweetly putting you on, a la Lily Tomlin. She has sleepily greeted the late-arriving visitor at their tiny one-bedroom condo, calmed down her excitable cocker spaniel, Woodstock, and graciously retreated, leaving the discussion going on into the hot, dry night.

Tom and Ruth Wysocki are perhaps prototypes of champion runners of tomorrow. Tom, 6th in the 1980 Olympic 10K trials in 28:19, has held several jobs since graduating from University of Nevada at Reno, but all of them has been connected in some way with running. He went from doing PR work for a Vegas Casino (arranged through running contacts), to the Sub Four apparel company, to Asics Tiger, to Brooks. Though he has been running seriously the whole time, he hasn't skipped a beat, employment-wise. Even the Brooks position was lined up before he left Tiger.

Ruth, who works for a computer parts firm, is a product of the intense Southern California age-group track system: "I don't even think about running anymore," she said. "I've been doing it since I was nine years old." In 1978 she was the national 800-meter champ in 2:01.9, ranked number one in the country in that event.

The day after our late-night talk, Tom and I picked her up at her job and went out for lunch. The idea was to get the *People* magazine aspect of this thing over as painlessly as possible.

I have seen otherwise "normal" households under considerable strain because only one spouse was competing seriously. I wondered if the Wysockis had worried about the volatility of having two training athletes in the family (with specific reference to the emotional break-up of Ron Tabb and Mary Decker, in which there was talk of gunplay). Had that been a matter of concern before they took the big leap?

"We talked a little bit about the potential problems," Tom said. "Particularly the jealousy thing: what if one person is doing well and the other is in a slump. We decided we would be able to handle that. I know that if she won the nationals, I'd be extremely happy, and I hope she'd feel the same way. But the bottom line is that our relationship goes deeper than athletics."

"Actually, we didn't really talk about it a whole lot," Ruth giggled. "We decided on Monday and got married on Friday."

They chalked the Decker/Tabb imbroglio up to personalities. They are in a position to know. It tells you a little something about the small-town aspects of being an elite runner in this country to find out that Tom has dated Mary Decker a few times and Ruth has been competing against her since childhood. They both know Tabb.

The Wysockis do not find their situation all that unique.

"Running couples are becoming more common," Tom said. "You've got Ken Martin and his wife, Lisa. Ron and Sue Addison. Phil Kane and his wife Missy. Guy and Lee Arbogast. But its still pretty rare, when you think about it, I guess."

Ironically, the fact that they both train seriously does not mean they spend any more time together. If anything, the reverse is true.

"I'd say on the average we run together about once a

week," Ruth said. "In order for it to work at all it has to be a really good day for me and an easy day for him. The hard part is for him to slow down enough."

"But it's one time I get to get a word in edgewise," Tom offered slyly. Ruth giggled again.

They made it clear that as athletes they far more often go their separate ways. She rises early to get in her morning run alone. He runs later in the morning, then earlier in the afternoon. When she gets off work, she does a track workout with her coach, Vince O'Boyle at UC Irvine, or else a road workout in the hills around their condominium. If it is dark, he will accompany her in the car. When it comes time for competition or socializing, they are not much on the local road racing scene.

"There is a real social running scene for couples in this area. We really aren't much a part of it, though," Ruth said. "As a matter of fact we tend to do more socializing when we travel to races. A lot of that has to do with our work and travel situation. When the weekends come you just want to be together. Forget about running for awhile and be glad to be home."

"Vegetate in front of the TV," said Tom, "When I was traveling all the time with Tiger, that's all I wanted to do. Saturday morning you can go straight through from the Three Stooges to the Munsters to F-Troop to Gilligan's Island."

Despite the fact that their training fosters little togetherness, they both thought there were definite advantages to the situation.

"One of the ways it helps is that we go through alternating phases of support," Ruth said. "When we first went out together I had just had knee surgery. So I went through the whole thing from 'will I ever run again' and back up through the first rough stages of training. Then Tom went through a period when we was unhappy with his job. I think we're better able to understand each other and help."

"But there haven't been many problems. I haven't beaten

her up too many times," Tom said jovially. "Not that we don't have our disagreements. Like who gets to take a shower first on a cold day."

When it is suggested that problem is easily enough solved, he replied with a laugh: "I didn't say we didn't solve it."

"Rats," says Tom, "Ruth's gonna kill me." He's fiddling around with his video recorder, and the problem seems to be that a news special has thrown the timer off and he's missed taping a portion of "All My Children." It is an obsession he and Ruth share with their good friend, miler Steve Scott, and several other widely-traveled athletes.

"We're really fanatics about following our show, and we've managed to infect some others," Tom said. "One summer when we were competing in Europe either Steve or I would call back to the states every few days to check up on the plot."

Other than the video problem, is a relatively normal day for the Wysocki household, which is to say that things are barely under control. In order to make time to go over to El Segundo Beach for a late-scheduled photography session, Ruth will have to run after dark (with a bicycle escort). Because of that Tom has to call friend and chiropractor, John Koningh—a 4:01 miler who is a good friend and frequent rabbit for Steve Scott—in order to re-schedule both their afternoon workout and a later taco dinner.

"Hi," he said to the receptionist, "Is Johnny in? What? You mean he has other patients besides my wife?"

As he gets ready to drive to a nearby college for an interval session, he fields phone calls from friends and business acquaintances who have heard about his move to Brooks. Although the dust has barely cleared, the word has spread quickly. Already in the bedroom sits a large box of Brooks shoes and apparel, guaranteeing that neither he nor Ruth will need to be seen in public in anything that says "Tiger" on it.

"Whatever I'm in, Ruth's in," he said. "The idea is that I wouldn't be much of a spokesman for a company if I couldn't talk my own wife into wearing their stuff."

While at Sub Four, Wysocki had helped to assemble a venerable team of elite runners. Though generally scattered now, the names are far from obscure: Walker, Rose, Masback, Dave Long, Dave Murphy. Yet he has found working in promotions for companies involved financially with elite runners to generate something of a conflict from a competitive point of view: "You're dealing with this guy on a regular basis, so you know his personal problems, his injuries, you're concerned about him, and you obviously want him to do well. But then you go to race him and you want to kick his ass. Strange."

Also strange to him is the local running scene. "You could find four races within easy driving distance around here every Saturday," he said. "There are guys who drive to a race, leave their car running while they check out the competition, then drive on off to another one if there are too many studs around. If nobody's there, they stay and run for the hardware." He has been fairly vocal about the insularity of the local competitive scene. He told a local reporter: "The Southern California running community thinks it's a lot better than it really is. We get our asses kicked outside Southern California. I don't consider it a big thing to be number one in Orange County."

"When you're in the business, you get these letters all the time in the promotions department: "I won the Kahanga Valley 10K blah blah blah. The worst are the triathletes. We used to get four or five a day from them. One guy in the department at Sub Four faked up a letter one time for fun and sent it to somebody else in the department. The guys couldn't tell it was a joke."

He rifles through a drawer and comes up with the letter. It is neat, maniac-style, pica-typed: "Dear Sir: My dog Blue and I are training for the Ironman Triathlon in Kona, Hawaii. Maybe you've seen it on ABC's Wide World of Sports? Blue and I was planning to compete in the man/dog division. . ." The writer and Blue were training upwards of nine hours a day and it suddenly occurred that what might give Blue and his owner a leg up (so to speak) on the competition would be a set of Gore-Tex man/dog rain gear.

Shirtless, Wysocki leans back on the couch in the warm apartment, patting his own, non-competitive pooch. He has sunk into that semi-dreading, black-humor-fatalism that seems to come an hour or so before a tough interval session.

"There are 2:15 marathoners out there who want $15,000 a year," he sighed.

"I've always thought the women were more intense," said Tom Wysocki. "If you notice when a track meet is over, all the guys get together and it's Miller time. But the women look like they still want to scratch each other's eyes out." We're at dinner and the Wysockis are on a well-worn topic: the difference between male and female competitive athletes.

"Oh, worse than that," said Ruth, "Even before the race starts, you see the men warming up together, joking around and so on. Until they are standing on that line, until the gun goes off, nobody looks all that serious about it. The women will tend to wait alone, warm up alone, do their sprints alone, eyes straight ahead . . . I'm not putting anyone down, I'm as bad as anyone." So intense has been the competitive atmosphere on the quarter-mile oval that she, like many track specialists, has found the roads relatively relaxing. She has had enough success to be attracted to the longer runs, and—again, as many track runners have found—the running public identifies far more easily with the roads. There are also some nifty rewards. The couple hopped in a "sweetheart" relay in Los Angeles and, despite a challenge from Barney and Jan Klecker, won a trip to Jamaica.

Unlike her husband, Ruth prefers a job totally unrelated to athletics. Yet even in her clerical position in the esoteric world of central processing units and ROM chips they know the hierarchy of the roads. "There was a fairly good runner who worked in a different department," she said. "He's a 39-minute

10K runner, and he was sort of the star of this little group around the office. One day he came by and you could see these guys winking at each other as they called him over to introduce him to me. They said, Oh, Ruth's a runner too.' Well, we talked about training a little bit and he was kind of patronizing and all. Then he said, And what's your 10K time?' I said 34:20. He didn't say another word. He just clammed up and walked off. The guys just loved it. They still talk about it."

But you pay some dues in order to get to play little jokes like that on the unwary. Ruth Wysocki has been competing on the track for 17 years. Her father, a 2:00 half-miler in college, had her on a starting line at age nine, where she ran her first ever 880 in 2:44. She ate it up with a big spoon. She was a "Valley Viking," the Southern California runner's equivalent of the Little League for girls. She was national age group record holder at age 11. She ran the mile in 5:00.1 at age 14. She won the AAU in 1978. She has run against some of the best female athletes in the world. When she talks about racing these days there is a tinge of wistfulness.

"I'm not really sure what my goals are anymore," she said. "I would like to get on the track this spring and try the 1500. But in some way, I'm not sure I really care all that much any more. About track, that is. Just training and running road races when I feel like it is different."

It does not take a genius to see that Ruth Wysocki's competitive fires do not burn as brightly as they once did. Not that she's not training hard, not that she's not dealing well with the injuries, the boredom, and the doubts that are part and parcel of the long uphill struggle. But there is a certain edge missing, a hunger no longer palpable. She knows as well as anyone that what she is undertaking is so difficult that without that kind of hunger one doesn't stand much of a chance. Though she says she is the kind of person who "likes not having enough time to do everything," perhaps she is secretly looking forward to that day when she won't have to come home from work, don running clothes and a reflective safety vest, go get five hard miles in the orange groves west of her apartment, and then breeze home and get dinner going.

The affection she lavishes on Woodstock as she leaves perhaps goes a little beyond that which is generally reserved for pets.

"I sometimes wonder what it will be like when the running is finally over for good," Tom said. "I mean, will we go out for five-milers together?" This is obviously new territory, an unexplored area that will have to be scouted, sooner or later, by some prototype couple. And when they get around to it, such a couple will have some other interesting contributions to make to athletics.

"We both want kids," said Tom. He looks at Ruth thoughtfully. "It will be very interesting to see the kind of genes they end up with."

Well, as it turned out, Ruth hadn't been quite as jaded as I intimated in this piece. In fact, this was written before she went out and shocked Mary Decker by winning the 1500 trials in 1984. She also made the team in the 800. She was back again in 1988, trying for the team one more time, finishing fourth in the 1500 trials. Tom has had stretches of good running on the roads, though has mostly been plagued with injuries. He's still with Brooks.

Update: Ruth is still in the news at age 37. As of this printing he made the 1995 US World Championship team, surviving to the finals of the 1500, then the following summer in the Atlanta Olympics, she once again wore a US uniform in the 1500 prelims.

When in Greece

When you think of the Olympics, what comes to your mind? People in little red jackets riding horsies over rows of bushes? Little girls dancing around with beach balls and strips of crepe paper? Two beaming women in waterproof make-up doing underwater splits to "Bolero?"

As an old track and field man, I can't help thinking of the Olympics first and foremost as the world's oldest track meet, and because of that I've always had a fascination and an affinity for the country where it all started 2760 years ago on a plain in the western Pelopennesus. A long-held dream was that one day I would travel to Greece, settle into a place in Athens, and then around dusk I would pull on a pair of running shorts and shoes and run up the hill to the Parthenon, there to commune with the spirits of the forebears of Western Civilization.

Well, I did travel to Greece recently. I settled into a place in Athens, pulled on my running shorts and shoes, and then ran up the hill to the Parthenon at dusk. But what I found myself communing with was several thousand modern Greeks with mufflerless Honda 50's and fire in their eyes.

After a few days in Athens I began to realize that the cradle of democracy long ago gave up ancient ideals of athletics and fitness in favor of a headlong pursuit of carbon monoxide and cholesterol. You can run for hours in the National Garden by the Temple of Olympic Zeus and, other than a few Athenians doing their wheezing lessons, you won't see the first runner or athlete of any kind. Even in the nearby stadium where the first Olympiad of the modern era was held in 1896, you are more likely to find kids riding their bikes on the cinder track and building sand castles in the long jump pit than athletes at their tasks. Such a laissez-faire attitude about exercise makes more sense when you realize that because of a lack of pollution control, the air in this ancient city is among the worst in the world. You can cut chunks of it out with a butcher knife and stack them on end.

The modern Greek approach to diet and lifestyle seem similarly designed to facilitate an early demise and a weighty coffin. Greeks are bustling, industrious people. They are up early, driving their mufflerless Honda 50's back and forth outside the hotel rooms of sleeping American tourists. The energy for this activity is provided by what the tour books describe as "the strong, aromatic Greek coffee" as in "Most restaurants serve 'American coffee,' but if you feel adventuresome, you might want to order the strong, aromatic Greek coffee." You might also want spend three sleepless nights pacing the hotel lobby, looking for someone to play Oh Hell with.

Somewhere around two in the afternoon, your average turbo-charged Greek, hankering for something with a little more body than liquid caffeine, will go out and eat all the lamb chops he can find. (This is no small feat. There are more sheep in Greece than cats, and there are a *lot* of cats.) Then he will fall into a profound and dreamless sleep (which even Greeks call "siestas") that will last the better part of the afternoon. Upon awakening, a cup of strong, aromatic Greek coffee will see him back to work until early evening, followed by a late dinner of many more lamb chops and perhaps a world-famous olive-oil drenched "Greek salad." Custom then requires that he sit at a table at one of the colorful outdoor "tavernas," conversing and arguing colorfully with friends and drinking ouzo until the pupils of his eyes look like pin pricks. And you wondered why in the movies when Greeks dance they always flap their arms like enraged flamingos. You try the same routine just once and see if you don't dance exactly the same way.

Somewhere around three or four in the morning, after a few hands of Oh Hell with the crazy American tourist in the hotel lobby, it's off to beddy bye. A couple of good solid hours of sleep and you're ready to repeat the process.

All of this has had a remarkably salutary affect on the overcrowding situation in Athens, a city of four million citizens and only three million muffler-less Honda 50's, where the average life expectancy has now dropped to somewhere in the vicinity of 19. In order to improve the situation even more, most Greeks have taken up cigarette smoking with their typical hell-bent enthusiasm. It is not at all unusual to find a typical Greek, sitting at a colorful outdoor taverna, a cup of strong aromatic Greek coffee and a glass of ouzo nearby, smoking several cigarettes at once, getting himself ready to dance.

Here are some helpful traveler's hints if you're contemplating a trip to smoggy and exotic Athens, where one can sit at a colorful outdoor "taverna" and observe the colorful swirl of pageantry and local colors as well as the ironic juxtaposition of ancient 2,000 year-old ruins set against the ironic setting of modern Honda 50's blah blah blah:

• Memorize the exact pronunciation and location of your hotel, as all of the street signs look like sororities you wouldn't want to join.

• You don't want to order your world famous "Greek Salad" with blue cheese dressing. If you do, Dimitri, the waiter, will just throw back his swarthy head and laugh at the crazy Americano. It's Thousand Island all the way. Bon Apetit.

• Personally, I would stay away from the strong aromatic Greek coffee unless you take along one of those little clown puzzles where you try to get the BB's in the eyes. Instead, I would suggest that you order "American coffee," which the colorful natives call "Nescafe," and which tastes faintly of lamb chops.

• Funny line to use on postcards home: "Dear Joe: Arrived Athens. Buildings crumbling. Please advise."

• Try not to be too impressed with the historical significance of Greece. Remember that in addition to inventing Western Civilization, the ancient Greeks also invented feta cheese, which no one has yet found a use for other than as fireproof flotation material for life jackets.

June, 1986

First edition note: Mary Ann and I actually had a wonderful time in Greece, though looking back I must say that Athens was just about as distressing a modern city as I described in this piece. The island of Santorini, however, was beautiful beyond my powers of description. Crete, with its Minoan ruins, rugged coast, and mountain ranges captivated both of us. We did our best to kill ourselves riding a motorcycle all over the place.

Ah, but just try to get away with a little humor when there are some real Americans around. This article was originally written as a column for Ultrasport. My editor, Chris Bergonzi (Hey, Chris, how's it going?), thought it was a little weird and asked me to do something else, which I did. Some time later, it was published in Footnotes, and naturally somebody who had just been to Greece took offense and wrote a scathing letter.

She made some pretty good points, too, but then completely blew her credibility by defending feta cheese.

To Imagine Victory

> ". . . They would have thought of this race
> countless times, some of them running it in bits
> and pieces during intervals or overdistance.
> They would have thought of creeping up to
> Denton's shoulder with a lap to go; that sort of
> fantasy could get them through long hours on
> the roads at night."
>
> —*Once A Runner*

There are doubtless very few runners who would deny occasionally fueling their training with the kind of high-octane mental imagery that has one entering the last 440 of a 10K at Jon Sinclair's worried heels. But fewer still ever elevated such glorious wishful thinking to the level of high art as did one Benny Vaughn, a sub-1:50 half-miler who was a favorite training partner of the Florida Track Clubbers of the early 70's. Benny not only conjured up wonderful fantasies, he shared them with all comers in a play-by-play commentary that found everyone in the group a "famous" foreign athlete, every training run an Olympic final, every telephone pole a finish line:

". . . and here they are ladies and gentlemen, entering the final lap just as they have circled each of the previous 23 laps in the Olympic 10,000 meter final: together. Now it only remains to be seen who will unleash his deadly kick first. Will it be Johannus Parkressa, the famous South African miler? Or will it be Benito Van Ness, the renowned Belgium cross-country champion, or will it be . . ."

In Benny's fantasy world, everyone was famous and everyone had an exotic foreign moniker. Everyone except Frank Shorter and Jack Bacheler, who, being famous enough in real life, got to keep their own names.

Although the runners were delighted by Benny's colorful and ever-changing vignettes (he let everyone win a gold medal occasionally) probably no one had any idea what future research on the human brain would tell us about Benny's kind of mind games: They are the very stuff that champions are made of.

Researchers are beginning to make quantum leaps forward in their understanding of man's oldest and most complex computer, the one that rides on his shoulders. *Newsweek* recently featured a cover story entitled "How the Brain Works," with all the obligatory four-color diagrams of neurons and dendrites; *Esquire* hopped right in with a well-researched piece called "Teaching the Brain New Tricks," (which featured distance runner Daric Donatelli's trick for remembering a series of 73 random digits: he associates groups of them with appropriate race times . . . and what miler would ever have trouble remembering, say 359?); and almost any day the week the newspaper wires will carry a story or two on new discoveries about which particular clump of gray matter does calculus and which remembers card tricks.

Much of this research focuses on or uses sports in one way or another. It makes sense; athletes represent, to the brain researcher, the most successful kind of interface between the chemical and electrical world of the imagination, and the sweat and blood world of physical motion. Very often what scientists find out in the laboratory only ratifies concepts well known to coaches and champion athletes for years. The use of fantasy or "imaging" is one such concept.

While most runners seem to fantasize during training, a random and very unscientific survey of world-class runners indicated that they approach the whole subject differently from the middle-of-the-pack runners. Psychologist William Morgan several years ago told us that the main mental differences between elite runners and non-elites during races was that elites did "associative" thinking (i.e. stayed in close contact with their bodies), and non-elites "disassociated," or thought of anything *but* what they were doing. The former obviously was a more efficient approach, and that efficiency was later demonstrated in the laboratory.

Morgan's categories, however, are not very helpful when it comes to discussing the mental processes at work during training. Garden-variety runners tend to go one of two directions mentally when training: they either disassociate and let their minds wander, or they associate and fantasize racing situations, using such thoughts to run harder.

Elite runners do their share of disassociative thinking as well, but they also do two very different kinds of associative thinking and they are very much aware of which is which. They fantasize about competitive situations just like other runners, but most agree that such imaging is almost always saved for the toughest workouts, such as interval sessions of the track. The other kind of associative concentration might be called "patterning," a process of focusing on some helpful image in a non-competitive way in order to improve the flow of the workout, enhance the stride, save energy, and generally run better. While some non-elite runners mentioned this kind of imaging, they didn't seem to draw a clear distinction between it and the competitive variety, and didn't indicate any inclination to limit competitive fantasies to particular workouts. Could it be that in addition to knowing their bodies better, world-class runners know their minds better as well?

Bill Rodgers comments are typical: "I can remember doing track workouts and thinking of Henry Rono's spectacular speed doing quarter-miles or halves." He laughs. "Sometimes it's a pretty disappointing comparison." But Rodgers said he still saved such images for his hardest workouts. He added:

"Sometimes I'll think about other runners in a different way. I often picture this one photo *Sports Illustrated* took of Jim Ryun in the wheat fields of Kansas, and another of Prefontaine in the mountains around Eugene. I can also remember one year when I was training for the New York marathon, doing back-to-back 170-mile weeks. I would go out on these 14-mile runs and I can remember really concentrating on getting through those long runs as intelligently and with as little wear and tear as possible. I found myself thinking of Abebe Bikila, and how his coach taught him to think of himself as being very light, just floating along the ground, and so on. I forget exactly what the words were, but they were just as picturesque as Muhammad Ali's 'float like a butterfly, sting like a bee.' " The other patterning fantasy Rodgers uses is a natural for anyone who has ever trained around bodies of water: seagulls.

"I will sometimes use an animal image," said Don Kardong. "Unfortunately, it's usually a slug." In a more serious moment, he agreed that fantasy played a big role in his training, and he made the same kinds of distinctions other elite runners made: "I use a lot of imaging, especially during interval sessions. I will place myself in a race setting, particularly toward the end of a workout, and occasionally I will think in terms of particular individuals. But there is a big difference between day-to-day mileage running and an interval workout. Generally you have to stay out of the racing mode, and that's easier said than done if you're running in a group that contains one of these guys who has to be half a stride ahead all the time."

"Usually if I fantasize about *anything* I'll run harder," said

Benji Durden, who does most of his training alone on Stone Mountain outside Atlanta. "But I don't fantasize about competitive situations very often. I've learned not to do it unless I actually want to run the workout that hard. A few days ago, though, I was doing intervals at a high-school track, and I was fantasizing most of the time. It's something you save for special occasions."

Durden also mentioned the kind of disassociative wandering near and dear to most runners' hearts (and brains): "Sometimes—usually when I wasn't really looking forward to the workout—I'll fantasize that I'm doing something other than training, like running from a pack of hounds, or running drugs into the country, something silly like that. That's always on days I'm not training hard, just playing.

"I tend to set up race situations, " said Frank Shorter. "Usually they will be fairly realistic ones. But towards the end of an interval workout I will try to focus in as if I were running a race right at that moment. I practice race-type concentration, but without setting up scenarios. I don't say: 'uh oh, here I am leading with a half a mile to go and so-and-so's catching me, so now what do I do . . . ' " And lest anyone think that purely disassociative thinking is just for the middle of the pack, Shorter added: "And, like most people I guess, I tend to think about pretty ladies."

But Shorter also pointed out that because he is daily involved in the *sturm und drang* of the business world, a portion of his fantasizing is of the "coping" variety, something he undoubtedly shares with many non-competitive runners. A comment of history professor Peter Ripley is perhaps typical: 'I haven't run more than three races is fifteen years, so my fantasies are rarely related to competition. What I fantasize about are the event of the day. I tell off the people who need telling off. I exorcise the demons of administrative living."

Some runners demand a great deal of specificity. One runner demanded more specificity when questioned about his running fantasies: "I think you need to break this down into uphill fantasies and downhill fantasies," said English professor Jerry Stern.

Somewhat typical of the indiscriminate use of race imaging is that of Bob Olds, a psychiatrist and good local North Florida runner: "I fantasize like crazy, all the time. Just the other day I saw an article in the paper about an upcoming marathon and that was all it took. The next few days I saw myself in great detail running that race, coming up through the pack, pulling away at some predetermined point. I mean, I saw every step of the race, street signs and all. And I'm not even planning to actually *run* in it."

Another psychiatrist has a different approach. Thaddeus Kastrabala, who pioneered the use of running for treating psychiatric problems, said: "Very often one can create a fantasy that helps one in training. I've done it often with patients. Finding out what the fantasy should be can be a fairly involved process because you have to understand an individual's make-up fairly well. What you're really looking for is a token animal. Usually something like a deer or an antelope, but for obese people maybe it will be something heavy like a bear or a bull."

Kastrabala said that the use of active imagination or fantasy is one of the fundamental techniques of psychotherapy, but that he had also used the technique of imaging to help one elite runner plan successfully for an important competition. The process involved physically going over the course of the race together, exploring the runner's past experiences, and deciding how to react to a variety of situations that might develop. In short, he led the runner step by step through the mental process that nearly every world-class runner goes through shortly before a major competition.

None of this is news to Dr. Ron Lawrence, professor of psychiatry and neurosurgery at the Neuropsychiatric Institute at UCLA, and founder and president of the American Medical Joggers Association. "Many of these ideas are akin to hypnotic techniques, but people seem to react better when you call it something like 'guided imagery.' This sort of thing has been around for a long, long time. I myself use it in a very studied fashion nowadays. If I'm going out for an 18-mile run, I will use a Tibetan image in which you see your body as a collection of separate molecules and actually envision the air rushing through your body until you literally become part of the wind. . ."

If you are beginning to piece together certain scenes from movies like Galipoli (What are your legs made of? Spring steel. What are you going to run like? Like a leopard. How fast are you going to run? Fast as the wind!) and Rocky III, (Eye of the Tiger, etc.), if you are starting to recall pole-vaulter Bob Mathias' exhortation to "throw your heart over the bar and your body will follow" or Marty Liquori's warning that "If you want to be a champion, you will have to win every race in your mind a hundred times before you win it in real life . . .", if all of this is taking on a familiar pattern, then well it should.

When champions over the years have told us that what they do is "90 percent mental," they weren't just modestly understating rather obvious physical gifts. They were trying to impart for free something of a formula they had paid dearly for.

Oriental philosophies and religions have contemplated such ideas since the beginning of recorded history, but Western man—excepting the occasional athlete, artist, or eccentric—has generally turned up his nose. Until recently, that is. Our scientists are beginning to close in on these concepts in their laboratories, and if there is one thing Western man is good at, it is catching things in test tubes.

For instance, Cornell psychologists Georgia Nigro and Ulric Neisser had a strange request for some of the students in their experiment. After throwing 24 darts at a board and having their scores compiled, the students were asked to "practice" dart throwing for a specified period of time, but they weren't furnished any darts. Or a board. Their "practice" was to be done mentally. Some of the students were asked to practice subjectively, that is, to imagine standing at the line, actually throwing the dart. Others were asked to stand outside their bodies watching themselves throwing. Each of those groups was broken down further into groups who were to imagine hitting the bull's-eye and groups who were to imagine missing the bull's-eye. All the groups then actually threw a series of darts and their scores were complied.

Results? The groups that did "mental practice" from a subjective point of view, whether they imagined themselves hitting or missing the bull's-eye, did statistically better than both the "outside watchers" and a control group that did no practice at all. After one more "mental practice" session, further improvement was noted.

Those who "practiced" hitting the bull's-eye, were scoring mean of 7.83 points higher than their first series, those who "practiced missing" the bull's-eye still scored a mean of 6.80 higher than their first series. The "observers" who saw themselves hitting bull's-eye were doing 3.11 points better; those who observed themselves missing did 2.89 points better. The control group improved only .28 points.

"Motivation is one component of the improved scores, but not all of it," said Dr. Neisser. "A portion of that improvement was actual increased skill. Something in those subjects' brains and/or nervous system was changed by mentally practicing."

Neisser believes the technique will be far more helpful in activities that do not require reacting to what someone else does: "It would be pretty difficult to mentally practice basketball," he said, "but on the other hand, it would be perfectly feasible for something like foul shooting."

Neisser has done no work with runners, but he is very interested in seeing whether mental practice might help Cornell sprinters smooth out their relay baton exchanges.

Darien Andreu, former Florida State University distance star, sits in the office of psychologist Carl Powers. She is wired, literally, for sound. Electrodes run from several fingers and various spots on her shoulders and connect her to a bank of machines that at first blush might be the components for the world's greatest stereo system.

"All right," says Dr. Powers, "Tighten your arm muscles." Darien's shoulders seem to rise slightly. Instantly a needle on one of the dials swings to the right and a steady low beeping tone becomes more shrill and faster paced.

"Now relax." Immediately the needle swings back down and the tone returns to normal.

Dr. Powers is a practitioner of biofeedback, which he uses at the FSU student counseling center to help students with the run of the mill counseling problems: depression, anxiety, obesity, and so on. His true passion, though, is the potential for using biofeedback to enhance athletic performance. His Ph.D. research demonstrated the kind of "open focus" associative concentration that good distance runners use during races can be taught to ordinary students in the laboratory by using biofeedback equipment. Then the skill could be transferred to the exercise field where it made the subjects demonstrably more efficient during exercise. He calls this type of concentration "open focus."

"When they are hooked up to the machines, they can tell instantly whether they are doing it right. The machine tells them when their heart rate goes up, when their temperature drops, when their muscle groups tense. After awhile, they learn to tell without the machines. Then it's just a matter of taking it out and using it."

Teaching someone like Darien Andreu, who has run 16:00 for 5000 meters seems like a coals to Newcastle proposition, but Dr. Powers plans to take this technique one step further with competitive athletes. He produces a chart entitled "Biofeedback Facilitation and Neuropsychological Images."

"Most people think behavior works like this," he points from a box marked "Like situations" to another marked "Behavior."

"Seems simple enough, right? You encounter some stimulus in life, you react. Except that's not what happens at all. What happens is that we encounter something in our life situation, we encode it in a higher language that our brain works with, namely an image, then we leaf through a whole stack of potentially appropriate response images. From these we select the most appropriate, and that image is plugged into our nervous system and causes the right muscles to move. All of it happens in a flash, so quickly we don't realize it has taken place."

Dr. Powers, a former college baseball player, a tennis instructor and a regular runner, believes that after an athlete has learned his "open focus" technique, he can then program himself to respond successfully in both training and competition, much in the manner that Dr. Kastrabala helped image his runner friend to win a race.

"It's not that we've come up with anything particularly new," said Dr. Powers. "As a matter of fact, what we're really doing is finding out what makes champions and then trying to teach it. We ask ourselves, what are the characteristics of a champion? One of the first things we come up with is: self-confidence. Now we have traditionally thought of self-confidence as something that comes from winning. You're confident you can win the game because you have won before." He shakes his head, pointing at the chart again.

"In actuality, we find that the champion was self-confident *before* he or she won even the first time. That image was somehow *already* in place, ready to be selected as the appropriate response when the crucial time came."

Although it is far too early to judge how well the technique is working with most of the dancers, swimmers, softball players and other athletes he is working with, Dr. Powers does seem to have one instant success story on his hands.

Quarter-miler Ovrill Dwyer-Brown has set school records her last two times out (600 meters: 1:28.9; 600 yds: 1:20.16). Although only in the program for six weeks, she is a believer:

"Up until I started working with Dr. Powers, I would never step out on the track thinking that I was going to win," she said. "I usually thought I had a chance, but he instilled in me the idea that I was the best runner on the track."

Assistant FSU track coach Al Schmidt has also been won over: "With some of these girls, it's almost like they have been reborn. Their whole attitude about racing has changed. Dr. Powers has made them very aware of the limitations they had been inadvertently placing on themselves. Somehow hearing that sort of thing from a third party is more effective than hearing it from your coach."

Hooking yourself up to a bunch of dials and beepers may seem like a pretty sterile way to go about paying your dues athletically, but Dr. Powers sees the process only in terms of untapped potential.

"We see some pretty high level athletes who don't believe in themselves. No matter how hard they work in training, the successful image isn't there in competition. They don't do well. Then they get down on themselves, and resolve to work even harder. Then they get hurt or sick and get even more down on themselves. It becomes self-perpetuating. Every coach has had experiences with the kid who tries too hard, the kid who does great in practice and miserably in games. They are the ones I think we can really help the most."

Whether his work helps bring us more exquisite ballerinas or faster runners remains to be seen. But none can deny that catching and harnessing man's elusive and recalcitrant fantasies is a noble quest. We should keep in mind, however, that every champion the world had yet seen has paid dearly for his or her excellence, in the traditional coin of blood, sweat, and tears.

And as yet one more psychiatrist, Carl Jung, once warned: "There is no coming to consciousness without pain."

May, 1983

Ghosts on the Trail

There is a running path at the University of Florida in Gainesville that goes down from the track past the law school, through a growth of cool woods, down around the married student housing area, around by Lake Alice, back up through Beta Woods (an old necking spot). past fraternity row and back to the track. It is a scant three miles and in the late 60's and early 70's, before all the joggers came, it was called "the warn-up loop" by the early Florida track club runners, who used to lope around its circuit every afternoon, talking, laughing and letting loose for the day's serious workout. These were the days before running had been "discovered" by America's managerial and professional elite, and thus we were accustomed to being regularly cat-called to by motorists and ignored by everyone else.

If as Joan Didion says, "certain places seem to exist mainly because someone has written about them," then I will take whatever credit or blame may be my due for the existence of this little trail. It was here that the fictional Quenton Cassidy, Jerry Mizner and their teammates jogged before practice, here in fact that Cassidy warmed up before stepping out on the track to meet his fate in my novel, *Once a Runner.*

But this path hardly needs fiction to spin its legends, for in real life it is, well worn by the great and never will be great runners who have trod it over the years. Runners like Jack Bacheler ran this trail. Bacheler, at 6-7 a giant in every sense of the word among the distance runners of his day, was a finalist in the 5000 in Mexico City and finished ninth in the marathon in Munich four years later. For a while there in 1967 and 1968. Bacheler *was* the Florida Track Club. There literally weren't any other members. When the rest of us came along, to say we followed in his footsteps doesn't quite tell the story. Jack had in fact made up this trail himself, had designated it a proper warm-up course, and that seemed good enough for just about everyone. We all ran it at least once every day the sun came up, and the days it didn't as well. Runners like Marty Liquori, one of the top miles and 5000-meter men of all time, pride of Villanova, vanquisher of Jim Ryun, ran this loop. Liquori, his dreams of Olympic glory now twice dashed—once by a betraying hamstring and once by global politics—padded the loop every day for the several years he spent in serious training in Gainesville. Now a businessman in town, he still makes it around the path every so often.

And there were others, too. Runners like Barry Brown, an internationally known steeplechaser and to this day a feared road racer; and Dick Buerkle, America's top 5000-meter man in Montreal an former world record holder for the indoor mile.

And somewhere nestled securely in the middle of the pack was your writer, who nipped at the heels of those greats, settling occasionally for a dual meet victory in the mile against much less fearsome college competition, but always humbly taking my seconds and thirds and fourths (and worse) at the hands of The Holy Ones who, because of better metabolism, superior capillary systems, better eating habits, or God-knows what, were and always would be my betters on a quarter-mile Tartan oval.

Surely there is a lesson in the fact that, of all these undeniably talented athletes, only a few survived to the very top, up there to that place of rarefied atmosphere where, if the runner maintains his courage and refuses to falter one final time, he may be able to stretch his endurance and spirit one more fraction of a centimeter in the final straightaway and pluck from the Olympian heights that most delectable and irreversible signal of singular greatness: the Gold Medal. It is, in the end, a sad quest. Sad simply because there are so many whose truly worthy ambitions go unrequited.

Who, of those who lead cloistered lives, fun upwards of 20 miles a day, literally make a religion of running, who suffer and conquer the injuries, the disappointments, the fears, who placate the fed-up spouses and relatives, who among them "deserves" to fail?

So, the ones who do not somehow "make it" take considerable satisfaction in the sweet victories of those with whom we have shared the pain, the toil and the spiritual blending of wills that is the result of having run 100 miles a week with someone for as long as you can remember. They become our personal champions, our better selves, the embodiment of what we would have done had we been luckier, more courageous, or purer of heart.

It tells you a great deal about the ferocity of the specters that haunt our little trail in Gainesville to learn that none of the runners thus far mentioned is the true ambassador of that path. Its unchallenged champion is none other than Frank Shorter himself, whose silky stride graced the circuit hundreds of times during the five years he attended law school in Gainesville.

It was that trail Frank left when he journeyed to Munich to write his name in the books of Olympus, and it was to the same dusty path he returned when all the hoopla was over. "It was nice to have something familiar to come back to," he said. "Most of the others didn't."

Four years after Munich I sat in front of a television screen in South Florida and watched as Frank tried to do it once again in the dismal rainy streets of Montreal. It was then I learned that if we are allowed to partake of the sweetness of victory then we also must lay claim to some share of the pain to which our fellow spirits are heir.

On the screen in front of me it all played out: There was Frank, all right, running strained but still smoothly into the stadium. But something was incredibly wrong with the scenario. He was irreconcilably in second place. he made a helpless little shrug (to whom? Louise, his wife, in the stands?) that seemed to say: Sorry. This is all there is.

If one misted up slightly then, there was no trace of shame in the gloss. Nor of empathetic regret. The same dew blurred vision four years earlier as Frank floated gracefully onto the track at Munich and upon completing the final quarter mile of his toil, put his hands to his head as if in supplication. He was indicating that it would take awhile for it to sink in that he had really done it.

Now that Waldemar Cierpinski had bested him that rainy day in Montreal would his life lack a certain symmetry?

The runner, despite being so much analyzed, interviewed and otherwise poked at and evaluated, is still a much misunderstood athlete. He seems to stir dark and ambivalent emotions in the spectator in much the same way a prize fighter does. In those athletic contests that pit force against force (whether brute strength or animal endurance), the populace delights in rapidly distinguishing between the heroes and the hoboes. There is, apparently, no middle ground for simple pride in being a truly incredible specimen.

Normal Mailer has said that in no other sporting contest can a man be so humiliated as in the prize ring. But observe how impotent the 3:55 miler looks as he struggles in behind the victor's 3:49. This formidable athlete, who would have been but a few years ago the best in the history of the race, now appears childlike *as he is beaten by 50 yards.*

It would had been a storybook tale had Frank won a second gold in Montreal, because he had become something of an articulate spokesman for the runner. From his thoughtful comments, it seemed, people were beginning to understand—even through the myopic and jaded translation of the sports writers—something of the nobility, the serenity of the distance runner.

But there was something eerily appropriate in his coming in second, for he had always said that in the marathon, the runner thinks less in terms of beating others than in simply running the best he has within himself. The project is simply too awesome to simplify to the mean confines of a *mano a mano* contest. For years, the public had demanded just that kind of simplicity in athletics (leaving the arena you could say of your man: "God, he's great!" or "God, he's a bum!" depending on whether he had met your expectations).

Somewhere along the way the American attitude about sport began changing. After 20 miles in the marathon, scientists tell us, man can run no more. He has no sugar left in his system to burn. The body goes to exotic sources for energy: liver, pancreas, other dark corners give up their last. At this point in the race, the marathoner has six melancholy miles to go. Something about this cruel equation that struck the fancy of the over-achievers of the American middle class. Spectators struggled to identify with it. Some of the heartier souls began trying it out themselves. When the whole thing reached that strange critical mass in the media, the trendy went out and got the correct outfits and hopped in too. There are now people trying to run marathons who would be far better off taking brisk daily walks.

Although in training for shorter distances races I had often run far in excess of 100 miles a week, I still considered the marathon an aberration. I ran my first and last one 10 years ago. I can still vividly remember reaching a checkpoint late in the race and asking the official there: "What mile?" My meaning couldn't have been clearer.

He looked at me with a mixture of pity and understanding (had the question been gasped that painfully?). "This is twenty," he said. And then, very curiously, he touched my arm very gently, almost lovingly as I went by. War novelists speak of that same touch being bestowed by medics upon the newly wounded.

Right before the race in Montreal, Shorter estimated that during the seven years of preparation prior to the race, he would have missed perhaps a total of 15 days of training. Through holidays, rain, snow, personal troubles, family emergencies. Yes, and through lover's quarrels, summer colds, downright blue funk. The runner becomes finally, (and you can see this in the eyes) an expect at *lasting*.

The world class runner develops an inner toughness, a ferocity of spirit that must be carefully marshaled and rationed over the many days between one Olympics and the next. This is a controlled violence that the spectator does not see on the television screen: The smoothly rolling process as seen from the video distance is, close up, the firing and banging of pistons, the rasping of deeply drawn breaths, the animal concentration of the incredible effort of running a string of 26 miles in five minutes each. It is not a thing easily understood without some means of personally measuring yourself against it.

There is only one real way to prepare for such a task and that is to live as a runner, day in and day out, for a certain number of years and then hope that when the time comes, things will work as they are supposed to. Hope that when you had to let up training three months ago because of a strained knee, that well-intentioned lapse doesn't allow some fellow from Ethiopia to slip by in the last mile as you watch helplessly. Hope that something you had for breakfast, in the cruelest of haphazard ironies, doesn't paralyze your resolve with yet an extra quotient of pain. Is that any way to neutralize four years of your life—with an undercooked egg?

Those are the realities of life as the distance runner comes to know them. Thus, perhaps it was fitting that it should have been raining on that day in Montreal, that Frank should have found his legs knotting up from the downpour. Hadn't his extraordinary tolerance for heat helped him to win in Munich?

The gods of Olympus were once again squaring up the books. Saying perhaps: You of the flesh, take nothing for granted.

It wasn't long after that race that I sat in a crowded theater and watched an American audience do a curious and wonderful thing. The movie was the original "Rocky". Up on the screen old Rocky Balboa crunched and battered his way through 15 rounds of a fight that was impossible for him to win. It touched a strange place in the breast when he made them slash his swollen eyelids with a razor so he could see his opponent in the final rounds. But he made it. Bloody and swooning with fatigue, he stood at the end and sated his defiance and pride by his simple presence.

It was then that this American audience, this throng that so loves its undefiled winners, that so loathes the weakness of "losers," this crowd actually stood up and applauded for someone who had finished in second place.

Ah, Frank, I thought then. Perhaps they are beginning to understand.

And perhaps they may some day even understand why there are ghosts in Gainesville who will not quit their daily rounds. Spirits who know every tree and bush along a certain dusty three-mile path: There is the mighty Bacheler, of course, and the fearsome Liquori (what a kick he had!), and the other Olympian, Jeff Galloway, and quick Sammy Blair and strong Jerry Slavin. And the Jamaican half-miler Dyce, and the Irishman O'Keefe, and Brown and Buerkle. And don't ever forget the greatest so far, the two-time medalist Shorter, he still comes by here every afternoon. Every day they trod the familiar path, out from the track, past the law school, down through the cool woods. . . .

June, 1983

For Amy on the Trail, Watching

These sad old mountains mesmerize. The mysteries of a topographical map, or the poetry hidden in the tiny local phone book can put a writer into a melancholy trance.

A certain trail goes up through Sherwood Forest (really) to the old Feedrock Trail, which ascends on up to the Harmony Farms path. From there, you turn and make the long gentle descent to Thunder Lake; somewhere along the way you passed an old lost Confederate lead mine where round lead bullets were once processed for the purpose of puncturing Yankee gullets. Once around the lake is a rocky two miles, then on the trip back on the same trail everything will look entirely different. Thirteen miles without seeing a soul. And while you were gone, you ran from one Carolina down into the other and back; a primal traveler in a space/time warp.

Kids with double first names like Jim Lee and Leroy Bob trod these lanes, carting supplies in and the deadly lead marbles out, thinking their own solitary thoughts.

Had you felt adventurous, you could have taken a rougher path down to a place which is surely enchanted (though I haven't been there yet); it's called Raven Cliff falls. Sit quietly

for a few moments and see if you can think of a better name for
anything than Raven Cliff Falls. I am putting off my trek down
there for something, I don't know exactly what yet. Perhaps I
want to be ready to compose a short story on the way, something called "The Mists of Raven Cliff Falls." I haven't the
faintest idea what the story would be about, but when you have
a title like that, surely the words will have to tumble over
themselves and fall gently into place.

There is a lady who lives around here named Asiley
Tinsley (Az-i-lee Tinz-lee) who grows flowers and who you also
go to see if you happen to want some apples (I like to mention
that I need some apples just to hear people say her name).
Another lady is named Virginia Coldiron, and she says that
with a little more convincing I might get her out running some
(she is 70 or so). Someone's cousin comes to visit from
Charleston. Her name is Andrella, which, in Charleston is pronounced: Ayun-drulla.

"Ah, Ayun-drulla," I say, "I myself was born in
Chawlston."

"How long did you live they-uh?" she asks, "You don't
sound like you from Chawlston."

"About fifteen minutes," I confess sadly.

Thomas Wolfe strode these crags. And a long time ago
they put crazy old Zelda Fitzgerald up in a rubber room at a
place in Asheville. F. Scott (who was writing movies out in
Hollywood) would occasionally come to visit, but it must have
been very bad for him because he stopped coming after a while.
What was that line of Fitzgerald's that novelist Fred Exley
loved so much? Let me see how close If I can come from memory: "I have lost my capacity to hope on the little road that led
to Zelda's sanitarium." That's close enough. Anyway, Zelda
died there when the place burned up a long time ago. She was
a schizophrenic, you see, and had broken her own heart by trying to become a ballerina at a time when there were no ballerinas.

The treatment at the institution was very avant-garde for

the time: the patients were made to do lengthy aerobic exercise, long hikes in the hills and so forth (ah, there *is* precedent for preserving the remnants of sanity in this manner). But Zelda was there for years and finally died in the fire while F. Scott was still in California. You can be sure that the Zelda he mourned was the pretty little southern flirt he met as a young officer stationed in Montgomery, and not the drawn, haunted old lady grimly trudging up the red clay hills around Asheville.

This is an area, being farming country, where all life runs closer to the blood; some of the harsher realities are not so carefully packaged for the sensitive souls among us, and in some very basic ways children here grow up faster than city and suburb kids. Folks will wander over to a pig-killing for reasons they are not fully prepared to ponder. Nearly everyone has a compost heap.

The physical strength of the people here is as deceptive as the gentle ferocity of a miler. Two city muggers broke in to rob the 70-year-old uncle friend of mine. One of them chased the old fellow into the kitchen with a knife. The old mountain man glared at the thug from across the table, grabbed an old iron coffee pot and said (he stutters): "Y-y-y-you -c-c-can kill me, b-b-but you can't eat me."

Then he proceeded to beat the bloody hell out of both criminals. The policemen who took them away said they were washing gore out of the back of the patrol car for days (but they say it with a grim smile).

Chill fogs get caught up in unpopulated crags up here and sometimes an aging good old boy (perhaps suffering because he never really got himself to Atlanta or Raleigh to, you know, *make* something of himself) will, out of a general sense of ennui and a down home conviction that it is the right thing to do, get himself omniscient on the Kentucky product and pilot his raked and overpowered Chevy out into the lonely air of a ravine with a poetic name. In the Burt Reynolds movies everyone then crawls out of crushed windows and yuks it up. F. Scott would be amazed.

The thing is done, of course, with mirrors and the latest kind of Hollywood witchcraft. In real life the aftermath is more precisely like this: 100 proof whiskey mixes with random body fluids amidst broken glass and smoking metal, and sometimes nothing is found for weeks (a horrified backpacker will stumble upon insects at work).

Up on Feedrock there is supposed to be the remains of an old homestead cabin, though nothing much is left save some rusting barbed wire and some scattered stones which used to be a fireplace. In hushed tones someone will say: "A little girl is buried up there. Died of the yellow fever and they just buried her right there by the cabin. But that was a long time ago, of course." Her grave is marked by a simple pile of rocks, and that is perhaps exactly as it should be. I do not know her name; I have always imagined it to be Amy.

One fall evening the runner glided quietly past the place very late on the way back up from Thunder Lake; it was raining and the dense woods had become lonely, wet and primal again. And probably so had the runner. There was not the first hint of civilization visible for miles (even the barbed wire is hidden in the undergrowth).

It suddenly struck me that her life much have been very hard out here on the side of the mountain. Hard enough indeed to leave her in that forgotten grave with only whispers for an epitaph.

Perhaps the strain of the 13-mile run was upon me, but I felt eerily close to her for a moment then, a tendril of sorrow reaching across the years, binding us for a moment in the mood of that deserted place where she had once played with crude toys outside the house her father had built of pine longs.

Whether from the rain or the mood, there were chill bumps on the back of my neck as I slipped by the place and headed down towards home, understanding perhaps more than I wanted to about cabins that no longer stand and little girls who never stop watching certain forest trails.

A bit later I mentioned the experience to Carolyn and

Jerry, friends who own Harmony Farms up on the same mountain. Jerry said he had had the same feeling around the place. And Carolyn said that a friend of hers with supposedly psychic sensitivity had visited them last year and told them that the hilltop was roiling with restless shades: "Bad feelings, she told us, Indian massacres, bushwhackings; a lot of bad feelings up there," Carolyn said.

"The Little girl," I said. "Did she say anything about her?"

"Oh yes. She said she was always up there and she never strays very far from the grave."

Ah well, I don't believe in that kind of stuff anyway. And I don't suppose you do either. Do you?

These old hills sometimes make for clear notions. You put up your vegetables in the summer, you split your firewood in the fall, and sometimes you die in the same bed you were born in. Folks are accustomed to looking you in the eye and making certain decisions quickly.

For some reason when they look into the eyes of a passing runner, they seem to see something there which is very familiar to them.

And when the runner looks deeply into the eyes of these sad old hills, he too sees something altogether familiar.

January, 1979

Living and Dying
in Three-Quarter Time

Z had a friend fly us over to the Bahamas in his twin-engine Aztec on a beautiful, crisp, clear, November Saturday morning. It was a day made of blues and greens.

From West Palm Beach the trip only took half an hour and it was something we did fairly regularly. Z was a stockbroker and Frates a fellow attorney. Only a few months earlier my interests had been much more land-oriented. I had been a member, with Olympians Frank Shorter, Jack Bacheler and Jeff Galloway, of the renowned Florida Track Club of the early 70's. Now I was a brand new lawyer and I had a new passion: skin diving, going deep into the sea with only the air in your lungs.

We got rooms at a funky little place called Pete's Motel in West End and then set out in a rented Boston Whaler to get dinner.

"Heigh Ho," said the powerful Frates, grinning from beneath his caterpillar mustache. He guided the boat.

"Beautiful!" said Z, sitting in the front getting his equipment ready. I said nothing as I savored the warm sun on my face. An occasional fleck of chilly white spray would land on

149

my bare arm and raise goose flesh. I had separated my shoulder a few days earlier in a flag football game and so I wasn't able to wear a wetsuit. It was going to be uncomfortably chilly in the water. Indeed, in a matter of hours I would be stone cold dead.

After thirty minutes of running in the little boat we found a good section of reef about two miles out from West End and set the hook. Z was a good skin diver. He could lie with his ample belly in the sand in 40 feet of water and shoot the eyes out of hog snappers. This is free diving, mind you. No scuba tanks.

I remember the water being very cold, and I remember having a hard time holding my Hawaiian sling, the underwater equivalent of a bow and arrow, using my weakened shoulder. But they tell me now that I did my part in putting some fish and lobster on the boat. The reason I cannot verify that is that the death haze lingers over that portion of my memory and I simply don't remember much of what happened that morning.

Strangely, I can recall vividly the one little scene in which I was enticed into oblivion. I was sitting in the boat, late in the afternoon, shivering with a towel around my shoulders. I was out of condition for diving and I knew it. It always seemed to take several days to get used to it, even if I was in good running shape. I hadn't been diving for a few months, and the chilly water had taken its toll. As I plunged back and forth from surface to sandy bottom in the course of the day's hunt the sea's icy fingers had slowly pulled and kneaded my body until there was nothing left. The pleasant self-satisfied feeling of well-deserved exhaustion was like the post-race oblivion much of road-racing America is now familiar. In a word, I was drained, flopped back in the boat, chatting quietly with Frates, who was also worn out. Z still thrashed around in the water, trying to put a few more pounds of fish in the boat. That was something I never liked about Z. He was always saying things like, "Let's go on over to the Bahamas and get a cooler of filets." That is how he reduced so much killing: a cooler of filets.

"Come on in Z, let's leave some for the next folks," I said.

He broke the surface gasping and excited.

"Man," he said, "Man, I have this giant grouper down here under a coral head and I can't get him out. My spear's still in him."

"Well, pull him out and let's go. We're cold as hell."

"Okay, okay." He gulped and disappeared. When he came back up, he was still excited.

"Come on Parker, get in here and help me get him. It's only 35 feet or so. He's 20, 25 pounds, at least."

"Z," I said wearily, "You are out of control. There is no way this deep diver is getting back in that water. I've just now gotten warm."

"Hey," he said. "Hey. One more fish and we go. This one is already nailed and I can't get him out."

A grouper is a strong, stubborn animal. It will wedge itself under a rock or a piece of coral when wounded. Even a small one can give a diver a hernia if it gets in a good spot. A topside fisherman knows to yank one off the bottom as quickly as possible after it hits a lure or bait. The skin diver's trick is to get two spears into one before beginning the tug-of-war, so if one comes out you still have a chance at the quarry.

I was adamantly opposed to the idea of getting back into the freezing water, I remember that very clearly. My shoulder still hurt, I was cold, and I knew only too well how complete my exhaustion was. But Z wouldn't quit. I looked over at Frates, who was watching this challenge with interest.

"It's going to ruin Z's reputation if I have to go in and pull his fish out of a hole for him," I said. It was the cocky athlete in me coming out. Frates laughed. We decided that I could wear Frates wetsuit top, which was far bigger than mine, and thus I could get my injured shoulder into it. But because it was looser it wouldn't be nearly so effective against the cold. I strapped on more lead chunks to my weight belt to make up for the extra buoyancy, grabbed my spear, cleared my ears and flipped backwards into the water as all divers do.

I went straight down to the coral head Z was floating

above. Looking up underneath it, at first I didn't see what he was talking about, there was so much sand and silt kicked up by his earlier struggles with the fish. But peering way up under the ledge into the deep shadows, I finally saw the large round eye of a truly enormous grouper. I marked his location and the angle at which he was wedged in, the automatic housekeeping of a hunter. Then I continued around the base of the coral head to check out the rest of it. Coral heads are like Easter baskets; I never could resist scampering around to see what Neptune had left: trumpet tritons, shovelnose lobsters, even an occasional sleeping nurse shark. I can't tell you how much I loved it. I felt so at home down there that danger rarely entered my mind.

On the opposite side of the coral head, I peered up under a deep ledge and stopped cold. Lying quite still and eyeing me suspiciously was the biggest grouper I had ever seen up close in my life. He must have weighed 50 pounds. He looked like a big, fat, camouflaged torpedo. My heart thumped involuntarily from the sheer excitement. It also thumped because I was out of air.

"It was the fact that you are a distance runner that got you killed in the first place," said Myrl Spivey, my doctor—and tennis buddy—two weeks later. "You don't panic uncontrollably like most people at the first sign of oxygen debt. You can override your system, tell yourself you have plenty of time even when you don't."

I surfaced next to Z gasping, and this time it was I who was excited. "There's the biggest damn fish down here I've ever . . ."

"Yeah!" said Z. "You see what I mean?"

"No, not yours! There's another one. A bigger one!" Z did not believe it. Frates, looking down at his watch, said: "You were down less than a minute." That should have been a warning. In good shape a two or even a three minute dive would have been normal.

"I was just scouting him," I told Frates. "I'm going down to get him."

I lay on the surface, face down, breathing regularly into the snorkel, relaxing as best I could to prepare for what I knew would be an enormous effort. I would have to go down and try to put this monster away with one shot and then drag him up, all in the same dive. The current, which we had been fighting all day, was getting worse. It made just staying in the same place a challenge.

I knew that lying flat in the sand, trying to shoot calmly up under a ledge at a difficult angle would be time-consuming and nerve-wracking. I knew I did not have much left in me for a clean-up dive, and we had no scuba gear with us. The idea of leaving a dying fish on the bottom with my spear in him repulsed me. I had an empathy and love for my quarry that only a hunter can feel. The Indians speak of these things but I do not think we understand them very well, sitting in our living rooms.

Some time during all this thinking and planning, I must have started hyperventilating. I don't remember doing it; I knew better. In free diving, unless you are diving strictly by a watch, you must avoid hyperventilating because it blows off all the carbon dioxide in your system. The carbon dioxide is what tells your brain that you need another breath. Your body is fooled into thinking that you don't need oxygen immediately. But your body is wrong.

I finally drew one last huge breath, flipped in the water and went straight down to the coral head. The next time I appeared on the surface I would be a cadaver, floating quietly, face down in the gentle wind chop.

I remember nothing of what I did then on that last dive. Perhaps I was setting up for the shot when I realized something was wrong. They said later that my spear was lying there on the bottom, harmless, the wooden handle having long since floated away on the current.

What was I thinking then, I often wonder. I can't really imagine myself as that dying diver looking up for the surface

that he knew he would never reach. Did I feel self-pity? Or perhaps a sense or irony that I was dying there in that quiet
blue-green world in which I had come to feel so eerily at
peace? It must have been a strange and poignant moment
down there when I finally realized that it had been my own
vanity and pride that had brought me there to a place where I
would blink one last time and then see no more.

But if I had been thinking about such things at the time, I
would not have been doing so passively. I would have been
scrambling all the while, saying perhaps, "If I can only get out
of this one, I swear to God, if I can only . . . " During that last
wild struggle, I did one important thing. I somehow reached
down and tripped the spring buckle on the weight belt, allowing the 12 pounds of deadly lead to fall to the bottom. At least
the corpse was going to float.

And float it did. Snorkel up, all in place except the missing
weight belt, my earthly remains bobbed in the waves while
Frates sat sipping a Heineken, wondering why I was having to
stalk the fish from the surface. He assumed that the grouper
had broken from his cover and I was following him, so normal
did my icy float look. He had no way of knowing that my lungs
were full of sea water, that I wasn't breathing.

As the current washed by the boat, something struck
Frates as unusual about the way I was floating, but he dismissed
it. I stayed like that for what he later said was "at least 10 minutes, probably more." The current carried me further and further from the boat. Then Z surfaced, sputtering, "Spear!" he
yelled. "His spear's on the bottom! And his weight belt!"
Frates' eerie feeling suddenly made complete sense to him, and
he was suddenly terrified.

"Oh Jesus, Jesus, Jesus," he said, as Z scrambled into the
boat. They slashed the anchor rope with a diving knife, started
the boat and roared out to overtake the body.

When they hauled it into the boat there wasn't much vanity left. Just sea water draining out in gushes.

"You want to know how you were?" Frates said later. He

spoke in his quiet, ironic, face-the-tragedy tone. (He is, like his father before him, a plaintiff's attorney, accustomed to dealing with hard facts of life: eyes gouged out by children at play, hands and arms lost to unfeeling factory machinery, loved ones lying under the wheels of drunken drivers.)

"Let me tell you how you were. You were dead. You were gone. You had no pulse, no heartbeat. You were gray. *There was seaweed in your teeth.*"

"Z wanted to just haul you back to the dock and call your relatives. He said: 'That's it for him. Even if we get him breathing again he'll have brain damage, so . . . " '

"No!" I said. I think there were real tears running down my cheek, as I sat in the hospital bed listening to him recount the story later. I was still having time-space orientation problems, as if I had been asleep for 20 years. Hearing him tell the story, I couldn't help rooting for myself.

"It's all right," Frates said gently. "We didn't let you go. Z did the hard part, the mouth-to-mouth. I got to work on your chest. You were so far gone that it took both of us to keep you going. We worked for 15 minutes before we got a little color back and a few minutes later we got a hand twitch. But when I stopped to try to steer the boat, you would start to lose color again, and fast. Finally we spotted a sailboat and hailed it. I was steering with one hand and doing your rib cage with the other. You started blowing lunch. Then Z would get sick. Then I would get sick. It was a lot of fun. But Z hung right in there. He volunteered to change jobs several times but I said no go. At this point we were still out by Sandy Cay, still a couple of miles from West End."

The sailboat people had a respiration tube, which makes artificial respiration easier and much more effective. Of even more help were the two extra sets of hands. Frates and Z had been keeping me alive, but just barely. Any slowdown in their efforts and I would start to fade. Since the sailboat was slower than the Whaler, a guy and girl from the boat hopped down into the little boat to help. The guy steered and the girl baled—the little boat was slowly sinking from the weight and the waves washing in. Frates and Z worked on me all the way in, but they were both beginning to sag. Frates' thick forearms were stiff from fatigue.

After what must have seemed an eternity, they reached the dock at the Jack Tar Hotel at West End. Then commenced a scene reminiscent of the movie *The Great Waldo Pepper*, when a bumpkin crowd gathers to watch a pilot burn to death in his crashed biplane. Frates and Z were still working like madmen down in the whaler while the entire hotel emptied onto the dock to watch.

"*Get a doctor!*" Frates screamed. Finally a vacationing Canadian physician emerged from the crowd of slack-jawed spectators and said: "I'm a doctor."

Weak with relief, the weary divers sat slumped over the dock. The doctor tentatively climbed down into the dinghy and proceeded to, of all things, slap my face. He kept inquiring: "Are you all right?" Since I was still very close to being dead at that point, it was a one-sided interrogation.

For awhile Frates and Z were content to sit around, sharing their adventure with the curious onlookers, but they slowly began to notice what was going on in the little boat and it became more and more obvious that the vacationing doctor had not the slightest idea what to do with a drowning victim. The doctor was still slapping the near-corpse around saying: "I don't think he is going to come around." And there was this: The color they had worked so hard to regain in my face was returning to the familiar blue-gray.

The idea that their herculean efforts would all be neutralized by some chance incompetence infuriated Frates. He jumped back into the boat and with a rough sweep of his arm pushed the confused doctor out of the way. "Get the hell out of here," he said. The menace in his voice and the cords standing out in his neck no doubt got a quick response. Though completely exhausted, they began the all-too-familiar routine, Frates pushing on my unresponsive chest while Z blew life into my lungs with the respirator tube.

It only then occurred to Frates as they slowly brought the color back that a doctor from Canada would know a hell of a lot more about frostbite than drowning. He now says the surrealism of the scene will stay with him always. During the long hours they kept me alive in the little boat out at sea, their only thought was that if they could only make it to shore, all would be well. Yet here they were, still frantically struggling to keep their friend alive in front of a crowd of hundreds of gaping tourists.

"It was a living nightmare," Frates said. "The crowd just stood there gawking. Not a single person acted as if they would or could do anything to help. We began thinking in terms of how long we could physically last."

Finally the sailboat people, who had inexplicably disappeared, returned. With them was a Philipino doctor from a nearby clinic. Frates wouldn't allow him down into the boat without a quick *voir dire*, as if he were probing the credentials of an expert witness in a jury trial. Had the doctor handled any drownings before? Yes, he had. How many? Too many to count. All right, said Frates wearily.

The doctor had brought with him a large oxygen bottle, which he began to administer. Finally an ambulance arrived to race to the hospital in Freeport.

I love the Caribbean islands, but that ambulance ride to Freeport was typical of a certain Bahamian style that in some circumstances gives pause. We had to stop three times; twice because the radiator overheated, and once (Frates swears to this) for gas. Observing such dubious efficiencies, and later discovering there was not in the whole of the hospital a single oxygen tent, Frates summoned our plane from the mainland and we got off the island the next morning.

Even then it was touchy. The plane flew only a few hundred feet above the Gulf Stream so that I wouldn't conk out from the thin air. I was by then conscious and theoretically rational. But I was like a computer that had only been given the simplest of programs. I knew my name and address and personal history, but I hadn't the slightest idea where I was or why.

"You were great to have a conversation with," Frates said. "You would sit there acting very normal and ask what happened. I would tell you the story, start to finish. Then you would sit there for a few seconds and think about it. You seemed to understand. Then you would turn back to me and say: 'Yeah, but tell me one thing. What happened to me?' Your memory span was about a minute. Z and I told you the story so many times we thought of printing up a little card which said: 'Your name is John Parker. You're an attorney. You have just drowned in a skin diving accident off West End, Grand Bahama Island.' "

"You couldn't even remember flying over there the day before. It all sounds pretty funny now, but at the time we were still wondering whether something in your head wasn't messed up permanently."

When the plane landed in West Palm Beach, I told Frates I wanted to go to my house.

"I'm perfectly fine," I told him.

"Sure you are. Every drop of blood in you is blue. You're going to the hospital."

The emergency room nurse was not about to admit this smiling, dazed young man—who otherwise seemed perfectly normal—to the hospital when there were actual sick people who needed beds. I like to try to imagine just how Frates would have acted. He had just spent most of the past 24 hours trying to keep a friend alive, and hardly anyone else he came into contact with seemed to give a damn. He would surely have looked like a grizzled, out-of-work commercial fisherman, holding me by the elbow to make sure I didn't wander off. He would surely have gathered some air in his formidable chest, fixed the officious little fireplug of a nurse with a glare, and then said something like "Look here, Miss. You put this guy in a room immediately. Get him in an oxygen tent and get someone to write him some antibiotics, his lungs are 80 per cent full of sea water. Then get Myrl Spivey down here STAT—call him at home—and get a neurosurgeon in here for a consult. You give me any more flap and come Monday morning I'll have you and the board of directors of this place up to your collective eyelids in depositions and exotic-sounding writs."

I like to think it went something like that, anyway. Whatever he told her, he managed to get his way pretty quickly. In his line of work Frates has learned his way around a hospital.

I remember very little of this tale myself. I have had to go back, as any other reporter would, to piece together the story of my demise. The first thing I can actually remember now is waking up in the hospital in West Palm Beach and looking around at a group of my friends. I looked over to Frates, ever faithful, and asked him what in the hell had happened to me. He rolled his eyes and joined the rest in laughter. This routine had become a standing joke. It was a joke I was not in on, however, and the puzzled look on my face merely added to their fun. By this time the neurosurgeon had told them the transient quality of my memory would slowly go away.

So Frates told me once more the story of my own death. But this time it was different. This time I remembered.

It has been nearly twenty years now since I died. I don't remember hanging above my body and watching disinterestedly as the others worked to save me. I don't remember long-departed friends and relatives greeting me and telling me they weren't ready for me yet. (I'm not saying none of that Reader's Digest stuff happened, just that I don't remember it.) And if I did have a conversation with God, He has elected not to leave me a transcript.

But I am changed in some respects. I understand as completely as a human being can understand what the Greeks meant by the word *hubris*. We don't have a comparable word in our language, but a rough translation would be: "fatal pride." I sometimes think that the whole of Western Civilization may be in very serious trouble for the lack of the word *hubris* in our vocabulary.

Others have pointed it out more eloquently than I: The athletes among us rush more quickly to the contest, more quickly to the war, more quickly to the other places where tragedy awaits mortal flesh. It was true in Herodotus' time, and it is true in the last quarter of the 20th century. I wouldn't have it any other way.

But I will never again take anything quite so much for granted. Not the resiliency of true friends, not the perfection of a rare skill, not even the very transient gift of life itself.

And I still search out those mornings made of blues and greens. I still seek out deep waters.

October 1979

Jungle Runner

B oogie" is a word he uses a lot. By that he means: run. "You squeeze off a round and then you boogie," he says. "One shot and then you better get two miles away as fast as you can."

"We can flat out deal in the jungle," he says. "Deal" is another word he uses a lot. The last time he did any dealing it was by swooping eye-level through ravines, tree-topping the green skin of terrain, raining a certain amount of death down into the leaves, attempting to win converts to the American point of view in the Southeast Asian, uh, situation. He was a friend of my youth and we used to run together before he went overseas.

Roger Morphus spent most of his Vietnam tour with his legs casually hanging out the side of a little Loach helicopter at 300 feet with an M-60 machine gun resting between his knees while the sad, broken, Oriental landscape of Vietnam passed below. Door gunner. Life expectancy: a minute and a half, give or take a heartbeat. It was a cliché of the era. Everyone has heard about that. In order to survive, he adopted a gunslinger mentality. The way to survive in the badlands is to become bad.

161

Now he finds himself in the Republic of Panama, sitting in a tree in the dark of night with a National Match M-14 and a starlight scope. A killer from a half a mile in nearly absolute darkness. His bullets are all separately weighed and balanced. They do not err. His scope is a miracle of optics. The light from a cigarette at 1,000 meters will illuminate not only the smoker but whoever is with him.

"Smoking is a bad habit to have in the jungle at night," says Roger Morphus. "When the guy takes a puff I can read you his dog tags." Roger Morphus is a sniper. His victims never even hear the sound of his rifle.

While the United States Congress very democratically debated and theorized, cajoled and traded votes around in an effort to decide what to do with the big ditch, a certain number of people in the Canal Zone went about their jungle routines paying scant attention. Dog soldiers; line dogs. Dogs of War. All they worry about is dealing in the jungle.

It didn't take long for sedentary college life to get to Roger after the Vietnam show closed down. There is something about the absolute blind-stoked adrenaline rush that comes from looking right into the barrel of someone who is shooting at you that finally makes any available stateside thrill seem just a little washed out.

"It's like looking at a harsh light. It hurts your eyes, you want to turn away from it. But you have to look at it because there is no place to hide and you have to take the guy out before he shoots you."

So you make yourself look at the harsh light.

One day in Vietnam they did shoot him, though. A fragment from an AK-47 tore through the engine firewall and ripped into his arm. He spent several weeks in a hospital in Saigon thinking it over. A few months later they blew up his knee and he figured someone was trying to tell him he'd stayed too long at the party. "I'm not going up again," he told his superiors. They knew he was serious. He came home, twice shot, defender of the Republic, duly decorated: a certified jungle killer. But his peculiar skills were of no use to anyone here. He was quickly bored through to his bones. Re-enlistment blues.

Now he's back in the jungle. "Panama is different from Nam," he said. "Not better, not worse. Different. Different jungle. When I'm away from it and start thinking about it—the snakes, the insects, the poisonous plants, the whole rotting pile of life a jungle is—it just gives me the willies. But when I'm there, I don't give it a second thought. Let me tell you, though, normal people don't know what the jungle really is. Two days in the jungle and you're eating bugs and howling at the moon."

He's with the 193rd. Alpha Four Ten. On the Atlantic side of the canal, they sometimes spend 20 days out of 30 in the jungle. The 82nd Airborne out of Ft. Bragg parachutes in occasionally for jungle practice and Roger and his buddies get to "aggress" against them.

"We steal their weapons, cut their patches off for souvenirs, leave them tied up to ant trees. Just generally mess around with them. We let them know they are in the jungle. Our jungle." The 82nd flies home missing some weapons and sleeve patches, but taking back with them a few cases of jungle rot, sunburn and some other problems better left unexamined. Roger says seriously: "Our motto is: 'Think dirty. Play dirty. And win.'"

Win against whom? Who the hell is in that jungle?

"Man," Roger rolls his eyes. "There are all kinds of people in the jungle. We don't even know who they are. There's really not much of a way to tell. Probably Cubans. Other Latins. Special Forces has a training school here for officers from other Latin American countries, believe it or not. We never know who's going to be out there. But we have seen them. And we have seen their weapons: AK-M's." The new version of the AK-47, which Roger is only too familiar with, is Russian or Czech-made. He says that each weapon makes its own sound and sparks a different emotion when he hears it. The AK report to him means imminent pain; a little like when normal folks hear a dentist's drill. Rogers always winces when he hears an AK.

But there is plenty to worry about in the jungle besides who else is there training. Even the frogs are poisonous. "The Golden Frogs of El Valle," says the post card, the poison from which ". . .is said to be used by the Matalone Indians in Columbia for making poison darts for their blowguns . . ."

"Matalone Indians in Columbia, hell," Roger scoffs. "That's chamber of commerce stuff. How about the Panamanian Indians of Panama?" Yes, he says, there are little people running around the jungle with poison darts and blowguns.

"We don't know much about them. We don't even know what they are called. We just called them the short little fuckers with the blowguns. They don't like *anybody*. What do they do? Hell, apparently they just run around all day shooting people with their damned poison darts. We stay the hell away from them." The jungle. A place where you stay away from things.

"Crazy old Adams," Roger says with a laugh, "Son of a bitch got himself bit by a bushmaster, this mean-as-hell, poisonous-as-hell snake. He was just leaning back on his hands in the elephant grass and one got him on the hand. Well, they Medivaced him out right away, but the funny thing was when they got him back to the hospital unit and put him on the table. See, he had this rainbow boa constrictor he had caught for a pet in his pack and the thing got loose while they were working on him. They don't even know one snake from another, those rear echelon types, so they all just jumped right on up on the table with poor old Adams." A little jungle humor there to lighten things up. Despite all the laughs in the emergency room, Adams pulled through. But the message is clear: In the jungle there are snakes to pet and snakes to kill you. Best to pay attention in the jungle.

The bushmasters are the worst, Roger says. They are mean; they'll go out of their way to get you. "They are a combination rattlesnake-water moccasin. They are big and they aren't afraid of anything." And then there are green mambas, not aggressive but deadly poisonous. Just watch they don't crawl into your shirt pocket for a snooze. And there is the fer-de-lance, pretty name, poisonous as they come. Roger has killed several. Oh yes, don't forget the sea snakes, also extremely poisonous. The salt sea holds grief for the unwary. Not for Roger: "I don't swim there."

And then there are ". . . ants, mosquitoes, sand fleas, ticks, bees, worms . . . so many different kinds of nasty shit I can't even think of them all; and you don't ever exactly get used to it. If you're lucky you get so you can deal with it." Deal.

He is there getting ready to deal with something, and he doesn't even know what it is. He is training in civilian riot control as well as jungle guerrilla warfare. He is trained to function in a mortar team as well as operate as a sniper/counter-sniper. He knows where the Panamanian gunboats are and where they are going if they leave. He knows how to sink them in a matter of minutes if he is told to.

But mostly he goes out into the jungle and deals. He hates to run anymore, because now he has to do it to save his life. One shot then boogie. Two miles. That's the life of a jungle runner for you. He trucks along in the shadowy mid-day moistness where he says your clothes start to rot off your body in a matter of hours. Nearly delirious from hours of hiking, or "boogying," he will fill his canteen from a stream and drink, not even caring when something wiggles around in his mouth. After a while he will seek out sunshine and just stand in a clearing for a few minutes to let the sun dry him out, because in the jungle he has begun to feel like he is rotting himself.

And then at night, he will sit in a tree and look at his target half a mile away in the pitch black. The starlight scope shows it clearly, a intimate little TV picture of someone ambling along a path, naively confident in the leafy darkness. "Bing," says Roger softly, squeezing off an imaginary shot. Then he relaxes and leans back in the tree. Waiting.

April, 1978

A World of Hurt

(One of the more poignant ghosts who haunted Gainesville and environs in the late sixties/early seventies was budding novelist and writing teacher Harry Crews. Though I didn't know him well, I often saw him running in the days when Gainesville had—aside from the university team— about three runners. It wasn't the only way he stood out from the crowd. He had just published his first novel. The Gospel Singer, a powerful, eerily moving novel set in the dream-like, demented Southern badlands. He has since written seven other novels, including The Gypsy's Curse, A Feast of Snakes, and Car. The latter is about a fellow who, for publicity reasons, undertakes to eat a Ford Mustang. One bolt at a time. Harry's novels are populated by the kind of people who are usually found handing out paper towels in restrooms: freaks, mutants, assorted amputees. I thus felt decidedly mixed emotions when he told me not long ago that he had admired the early Florida Track Club runners in those days and had seriously thought about approaching Frank Shorter to do a piece about him. I asked him why he hadn't. "Aw hell, the boy had paid his dues. I didn't want to bother him," he said. I had no such qualms about bothering Harry.)

Harry Crews is a picture of hurt. He has some kind of skin cancer across his face like a burglar's mask which he swabs daily with acid baths; there are knots the size of healthy oranges right below his knees; the rest of him is cut up and bruised seven ways from Sunday. He can barely walk. With his single gold loop earring, long raggedy dark hair, rough hewn features, and growly voice, he looks every inch a pirate on a losing streak. This inventory of bodily woes is more or less the result of an altercation at a dog fight (yes, dog fight) he was writing about for Esquire; a misunderstanding of some small dimension, you understand. A trifle, really.

As he explained it to Miami Herald writer Al Burt: "It was madness, man. The whiskey's out, the money's out. Lots of guys holding heat, lot of guys holding knives, lot of bullshit coming down. Two, three fights and the crowd's in a frenzy. Just madness. I just asked this guy, who was really a big guy—I would have never thought to fuck with him—I said, 'Hey man, you got a good shot of the pit. You can see. Just move over a little bit because you're in my way.' Maybe it was the tone of my voice, but that was all it took, man. Before I know it, I was on the ground and he was on the ground with me. He had three guys with him and they started coming."

"They weren't out to kill me," he said with something like admiration. "They were actually almost gentle. They laid me down like a baby."

Harry has had a way of getting himself into some kind of trouble in the course of just about every one of his forays into *reportage*, as most readers of his essays in *Esquire* and *Playboy* (now collected in a book called *Blood and Grits*) will attest. Indeed, it seems nearly every piece ends with Harry on the floor getting himself stomped nearly to death by someone making some kind of point or another.

Well, not *every* time. In "Going Down in Valdeez," a piece about the Alaskan pipeline, Harry writes about a legless man on one of those little rolling platforms. The man's expression is so blissful, Harry thinks he's some kind of saint or prophet, until the fellow rolls on off, leaving a small turd on the sidewalk in front of the writer. Later Harry falls in with an extremely successful whore and her ecstatic pimp husband, gets drunk and wakes up with a tattoo. On his elbow. A little *hinge* tattooed right there on the old elbow. Harry wasn't too happy about that, but it was probably better than getting the shit kicked out of him. This is his *non*-fiction, keep in mind.

He can't seem to understand why he gets caught in so many shitstorms without his hat. "I ain't ever been *in* Texas without being in jail," he told me in a bewildered tone. Harry Crews is a lively boy.

But if there is violence in the life and the writing of the man, it is not hard to discover its source. In *A Childhood, the Biography of a Place*, the story of his dirt-farm upbringing in rural Bacon County, Georgia, he makes it abundantly clear the kind of ferocity one can learn from the simple process of scratching a living out of practically nothing. That ferocity has marked him for life. In all of his writing there is the whiskey-laced, laid back, random, almost sultry violence which is the nearly private preserve of the Deep South. Occasionally there is gunplay.

It is from that Deep South that he clearly draws his juice. And much of his pain. I am not the first person to write about him who remarked upon the wonder that Harry Crews, 44, has survived this long. He is a walking confrontation.

But it would be typical writer's folly to try to explain the kind of hardship and violence that he has captured so movingly himself. The following is from *Childhood*. It is a crystal blue fall day; hog butchering time in south Georgia. The five-year-old Harry is playing in the yard with friends near the huge iron pot dug deep into the ground. In the pot the hog carcasses roll and boil:

> Out in the front of the house where the boiler

was, I was playing pop-the-whip as best I could
with my brother and several of my cousins. . .

I was popped loose and sent flying into the
steaming boiler of water beside a scalded, floating hog.

I remember everything about as clearly as I
remember anything that ever happened to me,
except the screaming. They say I screamed all
the way to town, but I cannot remember it. . .

What I remember is John C. Pace, a black man
whose daddy was also named John C. Pace,
reached right into the scalding water and pulled
me out and set me on my feet and stood back to
look at me. I did not fall but stood looking at
John and seeing in his face that I was dead. . .

But in that interminable time between John
pulling me out and my mother arriving in front
of me, I remember first the pain. It didn't begin
as bad pain, but rather like maybe sandspurs
under my clothes.

I reached over and touched my right hand with
my left, and the whole thing came off like a wet
glove. I mean, the, skin on top of my wrist and
the back of my hand, along with my fingernails,
and just turned loose and slid on down to the
ground. I could see my fingernails lying in the little puddle my flesh made on the ground in front
of me.

The old car that bounced Harry along the rutted
road to the doctor was so slow that Harry's
Uncle Alton "would jump out of the car and run
alongside it and helplessly scream for it to go
faster and then he would jump on the running
board until he couldn't stand it any longer and
then he would jump off again."

The scene is at once comic and pathetic, rendered with
precisely the same gentleness, sympathy, and humor with
which he tells most of the story. It is that loving voice that
allows us—perhaps for the first time—to understand and even
care about a people and a way of life most of us have long been
content to ignore or to actively loathe. This is the terrain of

rusted-out cars on concrete blocks in the back yards of baking-in-the-sun mobile homes, of "Jesus Saves," of Red Man Chew. Describing the poverty in a meaningful way was no small task. On the night that Harry's father died, a friend of the family came and stole all the meat out the family smokehouse. That's right a *friend*. Though he knows the thief's identity, to this day Harry cannot find it in his heart to condemn the man, so desperate was the day-to-day struggle to stay alive.

In such circumstances, paying the doctor real cash money would have been a heady luxury. And his services were required often. At the time he was scalded, Harry was only barely out of the sick bed from an early bout with polio. For months he had lain with his heels drawn painfully tight up against his buttocks, an enigma to the poor, frazzled country doctor. Auntie, the black old grandmother who helped tend him, told him his condition was caused by a wild bird spitting into his open mouth while he slept.

But it was during these months of convalescence he first heard the stories the womenfolk would tell while at their quilting. He would listen for hours. Later he would listen to the stories told by the men. He still remembers how markedly they differed. The women's stories were moralistic, flat, with characters of only two dimensions. They frightened him. The stories the men told were always about people they knew, were full of warmth and humanity, and were always funny in some way, even in tragedy. Harry and his playmates would later spend hours looking through the Sears, Roebuck catalogue, a strange and wonderful looking glass into another world where all the citizens, unlike the folks *he* knew, wore clean, attractive clothes and had all their teeth, fingers, legs and so on. The models in the catalogue seemed such fantasy creatures that Harry and his playmates would make up stories about them. This fellow with the golf clubs in the back is married to this lady up here in the brassiere. The older man with the shotgun is her father and he doesn't like the one she married. Like that.

Against the mean backdrop of this dirt-scratching existence the blessed escape of these stories fired both his imagination and his incredible ambition, drove him first to get out of there and get an education, drove him to the typewriter, drove him through ten incredible years of futile writing on speed while supporting his family teaching school, drove him to produce eight novels jammed to the covers with the southern gothic willies, and now threatens to drive him crazy.

It doesn't take long on the phone with him to realize that the man isn't even *thinking* about mellowing.

"Well, goddamn Coach, I guess I'm doing' all right. I mean, I been better, but I been a whole lot worse, too. I'm just sittin' here sippin' some wine tryin' to keep myself calmed down. I tried to eat sumpthin' a little while ago, but it didn't work out, you know?"

He was living at the time with a pretty girl named Maggie, who used to be a gymnast. Harry stays with Maggie when his wife, Sally, kicks him out. Since Harry and Sally have been married and divorced three times, it is a procedure with which all three parties seem vaguely comfortable.

"I think Sally's gonna take me back when she gets back from Salt Lake City in a few weeks," Harry says, with genuine enthusiasm.

It all sounds a whole lot more entertaining that it probably is, at least as far as Harry is concerned.

"My boy Byron was in the office the other day and we were talkin' and he teared up and I teared up. He said, 'Daddy, I know you got to do what you got to do, but does it have to be this *bad* all the time?' Hoo boy, that was rough." You don't need to know how rough it is because his voice clouds up and rumbles with emotion.

"Byron told me: 'Whatever troubles you and Mama have are between you and her. But if you ever need me, you just holler and I'll start walkin'.'" His voice clouds over again. Harry Crews does not live easily with his own ghosts and myths.

When he leaves the room for a moment, a quizzical look at Maggie is more than enough of a question. She begins quickly.

"He's been hurt this way for awhile, now. When he's hurt like this, he can't get around, can't run, can't exercise. He's put *that* away this afternoon." She said it as only a woman who puts up with a man who boozes too much can say it, with a mixture of gentle anger and sympathy. Harry's mama would have understood her tone very well; the men in his family "are bad to go to the bottle," as Harry says.

What he had nearly put away that afternoon was one of those magnums of Gallo Hearty Burgundy much cherished by associate professors, graduate students and other patrons of the cheap but palatable grape. When he really gets serious, he drinks the choice of the purist: vodka. And when he drinks it, he drinks a lot of it.

Such a practice often lands him in a hornet's nest of flashing blue lights, as it did one fateful night in St. Augustine. His offense? Well, some fellow in a bar had started moving in on Harry's girl and Harry had undertaken to urinate on the intruder's foot. The gesture had not gone over well. "I'm not proud of that," Harry said seriously. Like some other recent writers of fiction, Harry seems unable to decide where his fiction ends and his life begins. The vortex of such indecision, perhaps, is precisely the place in which the "legends" of the literati are spawned. If that is true, there doesn't appear to be anything easy or relaxing about it.

Harry occasionally suffers from attacks of the epistemological question and when he comes down with the godawful blue funk in some strange city has been known to go the library and look himself up in the card catalogue, just to make sure he exists. It is perhaps a function of such anxiety that he so often finds himself on some grimy linoleum floor somewhere, having the pure-t-hell kicked out of him. Both the procedure and the pain seem to provide him with some sort of vague reassurance that he is still around. But there is more to it than that. After you read Harry Crews' books, and after you talk to him for a while, you begin to realize that the *real* reason he goes out and gets himself hurt all the time is that deep down inside he believes he deserves it.

"You eat oysters?" He asks. That is the signal for Maggie to make preparations for the evening trip to the Windjammer Restaurant, a musky, softly lit place in which is perhaps easier to keep calmed down.

Inside, he is whispered about from behind hands; there is no question that he is being pointed out to the uninitiated. From beneath his fleshy eyebrows, Harry broods for awhile, then talks about a piece he is working on.

"It's for *Playgirl* magazine, their 'Man's Point of View' bit. Only a thousand words, not much you can do with that, but I'm gonna try." And how does the novelist view the current male/female, uh, situation?

"Hell, I'm all for 'em. I'm for ERA, equal pay, everything they want. I'm with 'em all the way, coach. But lemme say this. . ."He leans over and the right eye disappears under the fleshy brow. "When a woman walks down the street in a tight little thing and no bra and just kind of juttin' out all over the place, just don't ask me not to notice! I mean, ask me anything but *not* not to notice!"

"Harry actually reveres women," Maggie offers.

On the way out of the place, Harry is accosted by a grinning student who keeps pumping his hand, saying something about going out and drinking beer sometime.

"I've read everything you've ever written, you son of a bitch," the grinner says. Harry looks like that is just about the grandest thing he has heard all day and grins and pumps right back. On the way home, he admits miserably that he is going to have to take some pills to get any sleep. He has to be up the next day to go to either Oklahoma or Tampa, one or the other. So he sits, sips some more wine and contemplates with some weary relief the sleep that he has been working himself up to.

It is then the question is put to him. Is he happy, is he satisfied with the work that he has done thus far? He stares back with his pirate's glare, the right eye disappearing under the heavy brow. His voice rumbles again with guttural emotions:

"I think I do as good a work as anybody in the country right now, maybe even the world. *Yes,* I'm satisfied. I'm *goddamned* satisfied with my work." A pause then while he mulls something over.

"I think my fiction's far superior to my journalism, of course, but there's not much money in fiction. You do what you have to in this world, though. . ."

Maggie talks quietly for a few moments, and occasionally Harry's eyelids sag heavily and he drifts off. But he doesn't doze long. It is as if he is afraid that in sleep he will miss something. Or will get up and walk about in his slumber. Harry Crews knows something about paying dues.

It is easy to see that he will need those pills.

February, 1979

Bacheler Father

The mental picture lingers in my mind: the two of them are separated by a chain link fence, talking quietly in the hot spring Florida sunshine. The smaller one, an ivy league runner I had recently become friendly with, had wanted to meet my mentor and training partner, Jack Bacheler, a University of Florida graduate student. At 6-7, a finalist in the Mexico City Olympic 5000, Jack was easily the most exotic and arguably the best US distance runner of the era.

He was a giraffe-like creature, so shy that some people ironically thought him arrogant and unapproachable; my new friend was grateful for the introduction. We found him that afternoon, as usual, on the big grass field terraced one level above the track at the University of Florida, doing one of his endless, graceful interval workouts, and when he saw us standing at the fence he trotted over in his clipped little prance of a stride.

My undergraduate friend was every bit as soft-spoken and shy as Bacheler, and it seemed to me that they hit it off right away, if one can really judge such things about beings so diffident a smile becomes a display of rampant emotion.

In my memory they murmur to each other about the eso-

177

terica of training for only a few minutes in the glare of the descending sun, making arrangements to meet later on to talk. Then my friend and I leave to do our own workout.

"Gosh," my friend said, clearly awed. "Jack Bacheler!" I had just introduced Frank Shorter to his hero.

"You know," Shorter said recently, "over the years I have begun to realize just how much serendipity has to do with success. It's not like I was really smart and knew back then where I had to go. I was just lucky that I happened to go there."

But he wasn't the only one to gravitate gently into the Bacheler orbit; the man drew protégés like the golden chalice drew bored adventurers. By the time Shorter arrived back at the north Florida campus in the fall of 1969, Jack was already the nucleus of a small group of talented distance runners who would become known as the Florida Track Club. His contribution to the genesis of that group can hardly be overstated: he even designed the little orange logo now seen on hundreds of thousands of running singlets around the world.

In retrospect, it is not easy to describe what it was about Jack that attracted so many would-be stars. There was no bigger-than-life personality at work; he was no Cerutty or Lydiard or Bowerman. Just the opposite, in fact. He never lectured or pontificated, but rather taught by example. He was a scientist, going for his Ph.D. in entomology, the study of insects, and he brought his scientific objectivity to bear on most subjects, including training. He always prefaced his own ideas with the caveat that there were other legitimate approaches and that he certainly had not cornered the market on truth.

"I can't remember more than one or two times really *talking* about training with him," Shorter said. "Everything was learned by example, by watching him. He was always a moderating influence on me, just by being there; he was successful without running himself into the ground every day."

Little about Jack's early running would have indicated his later success. He was a 4:28 high school miler in Birmingham, Mich., a suburb of Detroit. At Miami of Ohio he was a good but not exceptional performer, clocking a 4:08 mile and an 8:58 steeplechase. Once he got to Gainesville, though, he began to put it all together. And he did it totally on his own.

"I remember when I first started running there in 1968," he laughs, "I was essentially on my own, and there was actually a period of time when I was literally running barefoot. I didn't have any training shoes."

And too, Gainesville was not the kind of hot bed of distance running interest that Eugene was even then: "I didn't see another single runner out in the morning for more than a year," he said incredulously. "Even after the Florida Track Club got going, we could have never *conceived* of what has happened to running in this country."

His training system was obviously sound, though "system" is perhaps too regimented a term, and those who wanted to be coached by him didn't even have to discuss it; they simply hopped in the workouts. It was the most egalitarian of societies. A law student friend of mine named David Block, a casual runner, jumped into a 10-miler one hot afternoon, inspired some mild curiosity about his identity, faltered along the way, and finally struggled in as night was falling, ashen-faced but filled with wisdom. Anyone could sign up, but tenure was granted only those who made all the workouts, the 7-9 miles at 6:30 in the morning at slower than 7-minute pace, and either a longer, faster run or else a bulky, untimed interval workout on the grass in the afternoon. We stayed away from the track enough so that occasional speed workouts or races were actually considered kind of treats. Jack thought that the 100-mile week was the mark of a serious runner, and that such a rigorous running schedule called for a partitioning of an athlete's life.

"He taught me two really important things," Shorter said. "One was how to turn it on and off. I think I still have that ability. He taught me that even as you're dressing out, you're still not running yet. Only when you take that first stride do you begin to get aggressive about it. And then when you're through, walk away and leave it alone. The other thing he taught me is that consistency is the key, period."

Most of the runners from those days, however, talk not so much about the wisdom of Jack's training or the glories of the Florida Track Club triumphs, but of the day-to-day camaraderie of the group. We had covered hundreds of miles together in that very special fellowship of folks doing something hard together, and we had become something of a rag-tag family. Because family members are permitted license not granted to outsiders, there was considerable badinage in the group, and the shy Bacheler, as at ease with his fellows as he was terrified of everyone else, was something of a ringleader. He never let Shorter forget who was the faster sprinter of the two, and thus poor Frank (who would later outsprint a gaggle of sub-four-minute milers—and Jack as well—to win the 1970 AAU 3-mile title) endured an unusual amount of hectoring for having "no kick."

Shorter was not one to suffer in silence and he quickly diagnosed Jack as an obsessive-compulsive personality, a worry wart so daffy ". . .he lands in a city and starts worrying right way about missing his return flight." Jack was delighted, and did all he could to encourage such play. Nearly everyone who trained with the group can remember at least once having to stop in the middle of a run, weak with laughter.

Jarrett Slavin, now a Tampa probation officer and cross country coach at the University of South Florida, was an early FTC runner and clearly remembers the general atmosphere of the afternoon runs. "A group of us once came up behind a sort of large girl in a bright yellow jumpsuit," he recalled, "Barry Brown blurted out: 'My god, a giant canary!' Jack was so embarrassed he crossed over to the other side of the street and wouldn't run with us."

But when it came to training, said Slavin ". . .everyone followed Jack around like little ducklings." It was serious business. A few months after joining the group, Shorter came back from a race to report: "The runners I know from college seems to look at me differently now, like I've moved to another level. . ."

Finally one afternoon when Shorter was away, came the ultimate recognition from Jack: "You know, Frank is starting to get pretty tough. I mean, you know, *really* tough. . .the little bastard."

It was the kind of pronouncement we would never have expected to hear from him about anyone *we* knew, and the combination of delight and exasperation in his voice marks in my mind the precise moment when Frank ethereally broke contact with the ordinary mortals in our little family and slipped out of sight over the next hill.

There were some early races when Jack and Frank finished 1-2, and then three races in which they entered the final straight together, looked over at each other, shrugged what-the-hell and, to the consternation of race officials, held hands and tied. They had put in so many hundreds of miles together neither had the heart to go for the kill.

To this day, Shorter says: "It was never a competition thing between Jack and I. We were just too close. There are two people I feel like I've never competed against; one is Kenny (Moore), and the other is Jack."

Moore finished fourth in the 1972 Olympic marathon in which Shorter claimed his gold medal. And Jack Bacheler, Shorter's former mentor, his training partner of hundreds of miles, the man he had been so pleased to meet through the chainlink fence that hot afternoon three years earlier, was also on the US Olympic marathon team. He finished 9th in the same race.

North Carolina State University Assistant Professor of entomology Jack Bacheler parked his incredibly dilapidated Volvo by the track at the Raleigh campus, unfolded himself from its interior and, dressed in running togs, began to do painful-looking bending exercises, fingertips reaching not much below the knee. His legs showed no sign whatever of disuse; they seemed to rise from the ground and attach somewhere in the vicinity of his earlobes. When two of his latest protégés, the tall and leggy Julie and Mary Shea, wandered over the effect was of a small convention of flamingoes.

⟶ Julie had just returned from the New York Marathon where a nagging hamstring injury had forced a drop-out at the four-mile mark. Jack had not wanted her to run at all, but she had had social commitments and swore solemnly to quit if she felt any pain. She seems, however, not particularly dour. If fact, she seems to glow as she approaches him, smiling, placing a tentative hand on his forearm ever so quickly, in the manner of a woman wanting to make a special point.

"Oh Jack," she said softly, "I'm in love." He greeted this intelligence with a look of mild discomfort and resignation, but seemed to know far better than to let loose one of his zingers. At 23, Julie will admit to going through a "teeny-bopper phase," delayed several years by the ardors of hard running.

"Is it always like this?" a visitor asked.

"Well, it's always manic," Jack said. "Either way up or way down." Julie giggled as the group started off on a 7-mile run. As always, Jack seemed to have attracted several local runners who train with the group and they were as welcome as any visiting world-class athlete would be. The banter hasn't changed much either. The topic of the day, once Julie's latest infatuation was played out, was her housekeeping. (Jack has more than once threatened to get a key from her apartment manager and let a piglet loose in the place.) She complained about all the clothes she had to iron.

"Here's what you do," Jack said helpfully, "You just lay all those clothes out flat on the floor and just let all those fat roaches run back and forth on them and stamp the wrinkles out."

"Oh, speaking of roaches," Julie said, "I caught this bug the other day and I saved it for you to identify. It looks like a roach, but it seemed like it was moving too slow. It was easy to catch. What do you think?"

"It still could be a roach," he said, a hint of the professor in his voice. "You know, roaches have varying degrees of ability just like humans. What we may have here is a case of a roach with no leg speed."

Nine o'clock the next morning finds Jack in a state-government car driving through the rural countryside outside Raleigh towards the billowing cotton fields where he will pick samples for an ongoing experiment. He teaches no regular classes; his entire professional life is spent in an apparently unending battle with the boll weevil, arch nemesis of the nation's cotton producers, and other cotton and soybean pests. Like most days when he is in the field, he was up before 7 a.m. to put in an easy 7 miles. This past fall he has turned in, at age 38, a 31:17 10K, and a 52:52 10 mile, good for second place overall at Lynchburg, Va. Such performances give him hope of returning to good shape after a seemingly futile seven-year effort to solve an agonizing hip problem. Never one to overstate an injury, he struggles to describe how serious a problem it was.

"This thing was so bad that I once jogged a couple of miles and had to spend two days in bed feeling like my hip socket was frozen in place. I went through five orthopedic surgeons over the years and, as a group, I have found that they are still relatively ineffective in dealing with runners' injuries. I finally was referred to an orthopedist at Duke named Frank Bassett who handles only referrals other doctors don't know what to make of. He was the only one who had ever seen this fairly rare metabolic condition before and thus was able to diagnose it. It's called "pseudo-gout," a build up of calcium pyrophosphate in the joint. He prescribed a really powerful anti-arthritic medicine called Indocin for it, and said I would probably have to take the stuff for the rest of my life." But Jack was able to ween himself off the drug after several months and soon was enjoying a pleasure denied to him for seven years: he was running again, and he wasn't in pain every step of the way. He had almost missed the boom he had more than a little to do with creating.

The path back to relatively good conditioning hasn't been easy for him, however, and he frequently uses the term "paying dues." Julie and Mary, with a mixture of humor and sympathy, tell the story about his running the Great Raleigh Road Race in 1981 wearing a mask the whole way because he was embarrassed by his rudimentary fitness. He was hard-put to outsprint Mary at the finish and claimed that the small mouth hole in the mask caused him to run in oxygen debt the whole way.

Like most of the members of the running community who have been around the block a few times, he ponders the physiological formulas of aging and conditioning.

"Obviously you're going to get to the point when you experience a slow but consistent decline because of age, and I'm sure it varies with the individual. But I believe that most of us, if we could remove ourselves from the normal pressures of job, family and so on, do nothing but eat right and think about training, we'd surprise ourselves by the improvement we could make. Barry Brown (now 38) seems to be running as well as he ever has, although I'm sure he can't run a 3:58 mile or an 8:26 steeplechase any more." As to where he himself might fit in the scheme of masters running, Jack will only say that if training is going well as of December 30, 1984, when he turns 40, "It could be pretty interesting."

"But with Julie and Mary training, I'm either going to be running along with them or else standing there holding a watch. And if you don't do a certain amount of quality, they are going to run you right into the ground. Once you get that far along with it, you might as well put a little more into it and get in competitive shape."

Jack has not only been coaching the Shea sisters, but also for the past year has been advising Dan Schlesinger, a Raleigh resident now at Harvard Law School, whose 2:11:54 3rd place at New York took the running world by nearly complete surprise. As usual, Jack takes great pains not to overstate his own contribution. "For all I know, he may be talking to ten people and sifting through for the best advice," Jack said.

"Oh, that's ridiculous," Schlesinger said later. "I rely on his advice above that of anyone else. He's been like a very old friend to me, as well as a coach. His advice so far has given me more success than I could ever have expected just by relying on myself, or on anyone else for that matter. I talk to him at least once a week, and I would like to do it more often than that, but I try to limit myself."

Jack strains so mightily for objectivity, it is occasionally difficult to discern his own point of view in an area of controversy. When describing the tiff that caused him to resign his part-time position with NC State's women's distance program last year (and subsequently caused Mary to voluntarily give up her senior year of eligibility in order to continue training with him), he prefaces nearly every remark with ". . .of course anything I say could be interpreted as biased. . ." He said he had been concerned about the way some of the athletes were treated by other coaches, and that because he wasn't usually allowed to travel to several big races despite a previous understanding, he had, in effect, been cut off from the runners he coached at a critical time.

"I simply told the head track coach how I felt, cleaned out my locker, and I thought that would be the end of it. Some time later, I got a letter, copied to the athletic director, acknowledging my resignation and saying that I hadn't been loyal to the program and that it was best for all concerned and so on."

Since he had coached Julie to All-American status 10 times, Mary four times, and Suzanne Gerrard once (as a freshman), had helped coach the cross country team to two National A.I.A.W. championships in 1979 and 1980, and a second place in track in 1980, and was named Runner's World Nurmi Award winner as women's coach of the year in 1980, one must wonder what constitutes loyalty these days?

Whatever becomes of the controversy, Jack will probably never square with the American ideal of the aggressive athletic coach. When Schlesinger wondered, for instance, which of the many offers to accept after his New York coming-out party, Jack's advice was to skip the glamorous foreign trips and the

local road races and to concentrate on his first year law studies
while putting his athletic energies into a good Boston
Marathon, so as to be seeded well for the Pan American Games
and the World Championships. Hardly the
"grab-it-while-you-can" attitude that seems to predominate the
value system of American athletics.

"I suppose it is not the kind of advice you would get from a
lot of coaches," said Jack, "Particularly if they were getting a
cut of the action."

But a fierce determination to do the right thing seems to
have a price tag these days and controversy follows him right
into the cotton fields. He has recently been caught in the middle of what might be called the Great Boll Weevil Brouhaha of
the 1980's, a political struggle over whether or not to institute
a multi-million dollar federal program to attempt to rid the
nation of the pest once and for all. The experiments Jack and
his colleagues have been helping to conduct make him think
the expectations for the program are exaggerated in light of
some of the evidence. Because he has insisted that science not
be replaced by wishful thinking, he has come under continuous
fire from the folks who want to wage all out war on the pest.

He parked the car beside a ragged looking cotton field and
began picking samples according to a random table provided by
a computer. This particular crop had been fairly well devastat-
ed by another pest, the worm, and he tossed the samples into a
plastic garbage bag with rueful satisfaction. The results seem to
be in line with his past research: eliminating the boll weevil,
although helpful, will not necessarily mean easy street for cotton farmers.

"Some proponents of this program would just like to
re-write my job description," he said, tossing the bags into the
back seat.

Heading back towards Raleigh, he is thinking of the afternoon workout. Julie has been ordered to the trainer for
ultra-sound on her hamstring; Mary will run a light interval
workout, varying according to how a potential cold is develop-

ing.

The girls' personalities present an interesting challenge for his analytical abilities. They are both products of the same strict, Catholic upbringing, but Julie seems somehow more tough-minded than Mary. Mary, in fact, is almost like a character out of a little girl's storybook. She spends a good deal of her time, according to Jack, "doing good deeds."

"She will spend an afternoon taking food to a poor family in Durham she has heard about," said Jack. "She spends a night a week working with prisoners, a night a week meeting with a church group, she teaches Sunday School, and so on. And she gives gifts to people. I couldn't figure out why she kept begging me to let her run in some little race last year, but I finally gave in and let her run the thing. It turned out they were awarding a color TV for first place and she wanted to give it to me. It's the one in the bedroom."

He drove past the Raleigh city limits sign in deep concentration.

"You know, those girls are sisters, and they are both really gutsy runners, but you'd be amazed at just how *different* they are," he said, apparently ruminating on some physiological or biomechanical comparison.

"Jeez, you can make cracks at Julie you couldn't begin to *think* of saying to Mary. . ."

Jeanne Bacheler seems hardly to have aged since the summer of 1968, when she accompanied her husband to the high attitude training camp at Lake Tahoe, hoping against hope that he would make the US Olympic team. Two Olympiads, uncounted national championships (both his and his charges), and two children later, the attractive brunette evidences only a kind of oriental serenity. The prospect of Jack's continued competition in the masters ranks does not fill her heart with song: "There is no use pretending it won't be a sacrifice, because it will," she said. "But on the other hand, there's no question in my mind that he's happier when he's running." Talented in mathematics, she is taking advanced courses in computer programming as well as holding down a job in that field at the university.

Despite an early and heartfelt protest, she was coerced into the kitchen to begin work on Jack's favorite dessert, an out-of this world butterscotch/cream cheese concoction which defies adequate description. She needed the early start. Soon the Bacheler household resembled a cross between a Norman Rockwell painting and Animal House. Sparky, the family's bee-eating mutt ("He's learned to roll his lips back so he doesn't get stung. It's kind of a hobby with him.")had gained entrance; Thirteen year-old son Matt, who looks more like a potential right tackle than a marathon man, was in the next room grimly practicing piano, and 9-year-old daughter Terry, the family's pretty, prima ballerina, lazily stretched a leg up onto a balustrade without the slightest trace of affectation.

"Want me to show you how to do that?" Jack asked, walking out to the patio with a tray of hamburgers to grill.

"Right, daddy," she said, rolling her eyes. She has seen her father many times straining mightily to touch his shins.

The Shea sisters, arriving for dinner, waded right into the melee, which that night included Jack's mother and father, down from Michigan for a few days. The girls are greeted familiarly and it is obvious they are very much at home at the Bachelers'.

Grandpa Bacheler, a retired commercial artist, had poured himself a little toddy and it quickly became apparent where his progeny might have picked up their verbal style. Needling, it would seem, is the family mode of communication. He had been laboring mightily all day in the backyard on a "tool shed" so elaborately built he has joked about renting it out as a house to a young couple with limited storage needs. With Jack in the cotton field most of the day, he had labored alone, and he wasn't going to let anyone forget it.

"You're really something," the elder Bacheler said to his son. "I can see now why nothing gets done around here."

"What do you mean? What do you mean?" Jack said,

feigning deep hurt and anger. "Just keep in mind most days while you're still warm and comfortable in your bed with two hours yet to sleep, I'm out there in the cold and dark running up those hills with tears streaming down my face."

"Right," said Grandpa.

Someone went to the refrigerator and found the freezer stuffed with plastic bags full of icy butterflies.

"Oh, those are the kids'," Jack said, by way of explanation.

"He is a constant nag," said Julie, picking at her lunch. She has apparently spent as much time trying to figure her coach out as he has her. "But what impresses me about him is that he doesn't try to vicariously live out his own frustrated jockhood through his athletes. And he is so much more intelligent than most of the other coaches I've seen. . ."

Their relationship, she said, got off to a rocky start. "When he started coaching the women's cross country team, I didn't understand his sort of sarcastic style _if that's what you call it. But then I started sassing him right back and we started getting along fine."

And too, nothing in her past experience had prepared her for Jack's approach to competition. During races he would always be standing a little ways off from the other coaches, who would usually be screaming at their runners. But when we passed by Jack, he would calmly say something like 'you're looking good, relax. . .' or something like that."

"Once, in my junior year, right before the national cross country meet, the pressure was really on us. We had gotten second the year before and Margaret Groos was all keyed up to race me for the individual title. I remember going to Jack really nervous and tense, saying 'what do I do if such an such happens, how fast do I go out, and on and on. . .'. Jack just looked at me and said: "Go out there and have fun.' "

The team won, and Julie won, but still it is not her favorite anecdote about Jack Bacheler. Her favorite story has nothing to do with racing, barely anything to do with running. She tells it, as athletes will do when trying to convey a vignette far more subtle than the primary colors of their vocabularies, with a slight wistfulness.

"It was in Seattle after the national cross country championships. We had done well, and were not only happy but just relieved to have it over. A few of us went for a long run; it was kind of an eerie, overcast day with Mt. Ranier in the background. There was something about the light that day, it gave everything a strange quality. Anyway, after we had gone pretty far, everyone turned back but Mary, Jack and 1. We finally came upon this old abandoned apple tree out in the middle of nowhere, just a really old, gnarled tree, but it had these wonderful fat apples up in the top of it. Jack climbed up in the tree and shook down a bunch of them. I don't know, maybe it was something about the light, but those apples just *glowed*. We started running around, gathering them up, stuffing them into our warm-up tops. But we tried to take too many, and while we were running back they started falling out and rolling around on the ground. We'd chase them and stuff them back in, but every time we got one in, two would fall out. Pretty soon the three of us were running in all different directions, laughing like little kids, chasing those darned apples. We just couldn't stop laughing."

"I don't know why I remember that so clearly," she said. "Maybe it was the light."

January, 1983

An Underdog for All Seasons

Benji Durden's pointy beard and sad, limpid eyes look vaguely familiar, yet it is not until a friend points it out that one realizes why. Benji is the real-life, flesh-and-blood version of Zonker Harris, that beautiful dreamer of Doonesburyland whose life's passion is the unlikely sport of professional sun tanning.

Not too many years ago, Benji's own *raison d'etre*, professional road racing, would have seemed just as esoteric and amusing. But while Benji will occasionally utter an ingenuous Zonker-like one-liner, the metaphor is somewhat limited. When cartoon characters step out into real life, they necessarily take on unexpected dimensions.

As with poets, rare-air mountain climbers, and other assorted brooders, fine runners tend to keep a certain counsel with their ghosts, and Benji receives his on the steep, leafy trails near his home in Stone Mountain, Georgia, just east of Atlanta. The selection of Stone Mountain was the perfect sort of compromise: Wife Barbara could easily get to her high-school art students, and Benji could easily get to the woodsy solitude where he entertains his visiting phantoms.

The meanest of his own personal spirits is the memory of

his college coach, Spec Towns, telling him as he left the track office for the last time: You'll never amount to anything. You're a quitter.

That baleful apparition is still with him, though he has now—among other things—run a marathon in 2:10:41, made the 1980 mythical US Olympic team, and banked $20,000 for a single pro-marathon victory.

But we love to wed ourselves to those early gloomy assessments, don't we? We cherish the deep hurt of those time-faded personal damnings. And we utterly fail to realize, most of us, that such pronouncements usually mean little more than: Your contribution to my cause has been a grave disappointment to me.

But Benji says with little irony: "Coach Townes deserves a lot of the credit for what I've accomplished by saying that to me." The lack of sarcasm is genuine. He is just a thesis short of a masters degree in psychology, and knows full well how such niggling phantoms, if they do not consume us first, may come to serve us.

This particular underdog has needed the impetus. When he graduated from the University of Georgia in 1973, his best track performance had been a 4:16 mile, and that had come during his freshman year. It had been a long downhill grind since then. He had had it with track. Why pursue an activity that was both painful and unproductive? But a friend got him out on the roads, doing some long runs. After a while, he jumped in some road races. He enjoyed it, but was far from an instant success.

For several years around Atlanta, the name Benji Durden meant a non-factor, a horse that wouldn't show. It didn't mean "quitter"—he was always hanging in there—but more the pathetic guy with no talent who didn't know when to quit taking himself seriously; he was a training bum. In 1976 he drove himself all over the South in search of races, an interstate highway system athlete.

Even now, after considerable demonstration of his talent, some of the old attitude still lingers, a prophet-in-his-own-country bias he has been unable to shake.

"A standard comment about me is: 'Durden isn't that good, he's self-made,' " Benji says with annoyance. "Maybe it's true that I'm self-made, but my 2:10 is as good as anyone else's 2:10."

His pique seems entirely justified. There are now on the running scene several dozen athletes with impressive pedigrees, times and racing records; in short, athletes who have arrived. Benji has also arrived, but he is unique among these other stars in that his point of embarkation clearly was left field. During his ascendancy as a competitor there were many times his fan club had a membership of one.

Of the thousands of interval workout burn-outs around the country, of all the talented high-school or college athletes who walked off the track after one 440 too many, Benji is one of the very few who has found his way back, not just to competition, but to the victory stand. And he has done it entirely on his own.

"A lot of the top runners don't like him," said Mike Caldwell, a long-time friend and the editor of *Racing South* magazine. "It's not the rank and file, the little guys; they love him. But the other top competitors seem jealous or something, and I think it's because Benji is pretty much of a one-man show. He doesn't owe anyone."

But while his pride and confidence are genuine, Benji is introspective enough to put his meteoric rise into perspective. The curse of a reputation as a plodder, he says, was also a blessing. It served as a buffer: Disappointments along the way were softened by the low expectations reserved for underdogs. Those surprising (to others) accomplishments, like finishing 11th at Boston in 1978 in a PR 2:15, were pure gravy.

"There is a good reason for my having kept at it long enough to make it. I have always been satisfied with where I was at any given moment," he says. "I knew enough to go at a pace I could live with; that has always been a strength. Guys like Salazar and Virgin probably would have quit if they hadn't been good when they were young." He thinks that over for a moment, then comes an insight: "I guess I've always been jealous of people like that."

There is an elfin quality to Benji that takes a while to pick up on, an unconventionality that manifests itself in many ways. He is semi-famous among top runners for the training technique of wearing several pairs of sweatsuits, even in warm weather. He has gone through stretches when he raced every weekend in place of doing speed work in training. He has also been known as something of a low-mileage trainer for a competitive class runner, hitting between 85 and 90 miles a week much of the time. Many of the people who laughed at his quaint ideas have fallen by the wayside, and that fact has not been lost on him. He has recently increased his mileage at the suggestion of Joe Catalano, husband-slash-coach of Patti, and credits that increase with several PR's, including his 2:10:41 at the Olympic marathon trials, and his 28:36 at last year's Peachtree. But the sweats and the frenetic racing schedule remain.

Benji is a player of games, a Rubic's Cube toter who says of himself: "People who sit on the john doing crossword puzzles have a lot in common with me." What they have in common is sitting on the john doing crossword puzzles. Benji is given to expressing himself in games theory: "Once I know the rules, I don't forget them." He means the real rules, as opposed to the ones posted for public consumption.

For instance, it took him a while to figure out the Athletics Congress (TAC) really wants to catch runners who take cash in the same way that your dog really wants to sink his teeth into a speeding Greyhound Scenicruiser. As with everything else, Benji has made his own way through the murky undergrowth of TAC policy.

"When I was just starting to get good, no one would tell me about getting free equipment, or how to negotiate with a race director, nothing. And there were guys around who had been through all that. They never told me anything."

His disdain for the hypocrisy and cant so endemic in road racing in those days led him to become one of the stalwarts of the Association of Road Racing Athletes (ARRA). "I didn't like living a lie," he said simply. And he is quick to point out that as a predominantly non-track runner, he felt he had little to lose by declaring his professionalism. The Olympic coin has been much devalued of late, and road races in other countries (except for Japan) were little enough to give up for a clear conscience, he felt. When TAC pretty much caved in and gave runners access, via trust accounts, to their own money, Benji was just about the only hold-out still insisting on open prize money. Finally, seeing it was utterly hopeless, he shrugged and went along with the charade.

During the days when the issue had still been in doubt, however, the vacillations of some of the other name runners had been less than courageous, and though he tried to find reasons to excuse and forgive, Benji was clearly hurt when he found himself being deserted, one by one. But although there was plenty of treachery in the struggle, and though he had reason enough for bitterness—being the one athlete who stood firm for principle through it all—one is hard put to find real resentment in him.

Don Kardong, former Olympic marathoner, said "Let me tell you a Benji story. Right after the Tokyo/New York Friendship Marathon, everyone was sitting in the auditorium while Adrian Paulen, the IAAF president, gave the obligatory long-winded oration. I was sitting there trying my darndest to pay attention, when I noticed this steady beep-beep sound coming from somewhere in the crowd. People were starting to look around, wondering what was going on. I looked over and sure enough, there was Benji right on the front row, totally oblivious, playing Space Invaders on his new digital watch."

Zonker holds forth.

"I'm bored a lot," said Benji Durden. "I watch a lot of TV,

read a lot of junk novels, a lot of science fiction. I'm into Ludlum, Heinlein, Follet, Niven." The infusion of cash had not changed much about the daily humdrum of the 18-mile-a-day runner. He doesn't even mind describing his status as that of a househusband, something he calls "part of the deal." Also part of the deal is getting up at 6:30 a.m. to make Barbara's lunch, something he has done for years. His wife is one of those serene, unflappable women one seems to find in the company of underdogs-made-good. Her only lament has been she could-n't always take time off for the longer trips.

"Once he was gone for a week and things really piled up," she said. "Things" meant the wash.

They live in the same comfortable, split-level two-bed-room home they have occupied for years, though the couple has now incorporated "for tax purposes." Benji and 2:15 marathoner neighbor Lee Fidler have started a runner con-sulting business whereby they envision counseling aspiring weekend road racers. Fidler's part in the project is described as "the hook." "I'm the bait, he's the hook," Benji says. He shows a visitor a flyer with the two runners pictured striding boldly atop a listing of their accomplishments. Among all the impres-sive titles and times is a claim that the duo have collected some 23 Peachtree T-shirts between them.

"Who knows," says Benji quizzically, "we put that in as sort of a joke, but to a lot of those folks out there it probably means more than a 2:10 in the marathon."

When it is suggested that he lives in a fantasy world far from the sound and fury of daily commerce, Benji says that to him, a life of running around Stone Mountain, doing the wash, and reading *Children of Dune*, seems entirely normal, and that when he hops on a plane at the nearby Atlanta airport to flit around the country and world in quest of his living, that is the real fantasy.

It is hard to know what constitutes a "normal" runner's life style anymore. On a recent weekend Benji headed up to Boston, ostensibly for a pro-circuit race, the Freedom Trail

Run, but since he was marathon-weary and his chances were slim, he mostly went because ARRA was holding meetings, and he could get in a visit with his close friends, Joe and Patti Catalano.

Arriving in Boston, he went directly to their apartment, which was in the process of being vacated in favor of a brand spanking new three-bedroom job in the upper middle-class suburbs.

The tiny apartment, typical runner digs of a past impoverished era, looked like nothing so much as an explosion in a trophy factory.

Patti stopped directing the demolition long enough to fling her arms around Benji's neck and welcome him to town. She then went back to the middle of the rubble, tiny hands on tiny hips, rolled her eyes in dismay at the scattered training shoes, rain gear, T-shirts, and the posters and mementoes of several hundred aerobic encounters.

"This a*pah*tment!" she wailed in dismay, picking up a cardboard box and scooping the entire contents of one cupboard (vitamins, lecithin, niacin, but leaving one tired looking jar of sunflower seed paste: "Yuk"). She bolted through the door and was gone.

Though the new Catalano dwelling is so new it seemed the Cellophane was still on it, Patti dismissed Benji's enthusiastic compliments: "Ah, Benj, we're only going to be here three to five years at the most." She and her coach have already picked out their next home site. The Catalanos are so upwardly mobile that unpacking seems almost a defeatist gesture.

Patti put down a box and gave Benji a knowing look. "And what have you bought, Benji?"

"Oh, nothing really. A video tape is all." He is a bit proud of his parsimony.

Two mornings later, Patti and Joe sat in a darkened theater watching a special screening of *Chariots of Fire.* Up on the screen Sir John Gielgud and Ben Cross bantered back and forth about the fine points of 1920's British amateurism in a manner that would have been credible up until a very few years ago: "Mr. Abrahams, we understand that you are being coached by a . . . *foreigner*." Translation: You are trying too hard, fellow. The point is to win, but to make it look easy as you do it. That is the way of the proper sporting gentleman. In the *persona* of TAC's former baroque amateur policies, the specter of such attitudes had haunted athletes up until very recently.

Patti Catalano, a 95-pound, tough-talking former chain smoker, watched the movie in a trance. She will make perhaps a quarter of a million dollars over the next several years with her own sporting ability, and her fascination was that of some-one eavesdropping on an ancient but immensely curious era: a paleontologist among the dinosaur bones.

Outside the theater, still enraptured by the movie, she began walking to the Parker House Hotel to meet Benji, who had to skip the movie because of ARRA meetings. It began to rain and Patti responded by trotting along the sidewalk. Unable to contain herself very long, the trot picked up speed even though she was wearing clumsy clogs. Finally, totally carried away, she began a joyful sprint through a crowd of impervious Bostonians and the whole thing became too much for her. Long flowing hair blowing out behind her, laughing gaily, she blurted out: "Two years ago we were on food stamps!"

As he had feared, the Freedom Trail race did not go well, and it was back to Stone Mountain, the laundry, Rubic's Cube and his private ghosts. He was not particularly disappointed. In fact, he was happy to have supported ARRA just by showing up. And he had given a deposition, as had Kardong and Ric Rojas, to an attorney for Paul Friedman, a defrocked former amateur who is challenging TAC in federal court in New York. The deposition had taken on the now familiar surrealistic tones. In answer to one question about whether TAC knew prize money was given at a certain race in Georgia, Benji replied: "It was a TAC official that handed me the check."

Kardong and Rojas gave similar testimony:

Question: What makes you think TAC had to know there was prize money at such-and-such race?

Answer: Because the prize schedule was printed in the paper.

But the Freedom Trail race had been troubling in at least one respect: it had been won by Rod Dixon, who was one of the first name runners to go along with the trust-account plan. It was the beginning of the end for ARRA's tough stand. If runners could have their cake and eat it too (i.e. take money and still technically be amateurs) just by jumping through some accounting hoops, chances were that most of them would go along with it.

A few weeks after the race, a troubled Benji Durden sat in front of his television set and watched with chagrin as Alberto Salazar ran his stunning world record New York Marathon. Benji, as a declared professional, couldn't compete because there were foreign athletes in the field. Back in Boston, Benji had engaged in a long argument with Jon Sinclair about whether Salazar could make good on his prediction of going under 2:08. Benji argued that he couldn't do it, but the Oregonian had come close enough to give Benji the shakes. After watching the televised race, Benji went right out and inadvertently shaved seven minutes off his normal 10-mile training time.

As he had told Patti Catalano, his one extravagant trinket was his $2,000 VCR, and almost anyone who comes to the house discovers that Benji will find an excuse to play his tape of Salazar's victory again and again.

"He probably made around $50,000 as a direct result of winning that race," said Benji, shaking his head. "Because he plays the game and takes it under the table."

"It is probably an irrational emotion, because I'm not at all certain I'm physically capable of running that fast, but I feel like Salazar has taken something away from me by breaking Clayton's record," he said.

Switching off the machine, he zipped up his sweat top and headed out the door to counsel with the ghosts on his Stone Mountain trail. "Sometimes the frustration of this whole thing builds up in me until I think I'm going to explode," he said.

But he doesn't. Instead, Zonker, that beautiful dreamer, simply slips off down the road and disappears into the autumn woods.

November, 1981

First edition note: Much water under the bridge. The reforms Benji and the others fought for have been, for all practical purposes, won. Serious runners are now able to earn a living by the expedient routing of money through a "trust account." It is, of course, a sham, but then so are the various races by which Iron Curtain countries support their athletes while allowing them to maintain their amateur standing.

Patti Catalano has been plagued by injuries and has struggled valiantly to come back. It hasn't happened as of this writing. Benji is now divorced from Barbara, lives in Nashville, and is helping to run Racing South Magazine, in which he has an interest. In the 1983 Boston Marathon, Benji led for much of the first 10 miles, faltered only slightly with a bad case of blisters, and finished third—in a personal best time of 2:09:58. No longer quite so underrated, he continued to be one of the top ranked runners in the country.

September, 1983

Second edition note: More water under the bridge, of course. Benji has now lived for several years in Boulder, where he cuts a wide swath with his goatee and his white linen suits. Unfortunately, he's been plagued by injuries and has never regained the shape he showed in Boston in '83. But he still runs mountain trails every day, plotting comebacks.

Patti Catalano has long been divorced from Joe. In an article in the May, 1988 Running Times she revealed the terrible battle she had long fought bulimia, which she has apparently now won. She lives quietly and happily in a small town in Vermont, where she co-manages a market and deli. She still runs, and has competed with some success recently.

September, 1988

Current edition note: Benji is still in Boulder and has achieved considerable success as a coach of elite runners, including Kim Jones. Patti is back in Boston, a happily married mother of one very energetic son.

The True Aerobic Believer

Even in that era of eccentricity J.F. Galloway was up to the challenge. A gray November Chicago morning in 1970 found the runners of the Florida Track Club performing their final warm-up rites before running six miles through the slush of Washington Park in quest of the national cross country title.

Frank Shorter, who then sported a little ponytail and a drooping Elliot Gould mustache, sat with Olympian teammate Jack Bacheler (rakish sideburns, cocky grin) while they applied Vaseline to their racing spikes in a futile attempt to keep their feet dry for at least a few minutes of the race. Someone jogged by and said that Galloway was going to wear Gladbags on his feet.

What?

That's right, Gladbags. Shorter and Bacheler looked at each other and shrugged. Well, that was ol' Jeff all right and no one was terribly surprised to find out that he would undertake to plow through six miles of Yankee mud in a pair of Gladbags. Even among this caste of eccentrics, the boy was known to be a little . . . different. There was the time when one of the shot-putters at the Olympic trials went a little crazy and ripped a

bunch of telephones off the dorm walls. Nothing would do but
that Galloway install one of them in his old rattletrap Volvo,
which he called "Mobley," in order to keep in touch with whatever spirits one communicates with on an inert phone.

"One night we pulled up at a light next to a guy in a
Mercedes who was talking on his car phone," recalled Bacheler.
"Galloway just reached over, took his phone off the hook, said
something into the mouthpiece, and then held it out the window to the Mercedes man. 'It's for you,' he told the guy."

Despite the antics, there was always something of the
Wide-Eyed True Believer about Jeff, a sort of religious quality
that transcended any known orthodoxy. He had the kinetic
energy of a buzz bomb, a good -nature intensity that allowed
him to bounce from one project to any of a hundred others, all
the while maintaining a certain serenity, an inner control. He
focused on people, fixing them with his big clear eyes that just
radiated *sincerity*. He really did care about your stress fracture
and wasn't just waiting politely for you to finish so he could lay
his own tale of woe on you.

And he had a thousand ideas. Never mind that on that
November morning the perspiration built up inside those funky
Gladbags until by the time he finished the race it was like he
was wearing a pair of water balloons on his feet. It was pure
Galloway and if it didn't work it was only because the Gladbag
people hadn't yet come up with a porous product suitable for
footwear. Since that day in Chicago (the Florida Track Club
lost by a few points) Galloway went on to run on the 1972
Olympic team (10,000), founded the Phidippides running store
chain, and was instrumental in turning the Peachtree Road
Race from a quilting bee into an annual spectacle of apocalyp-
tic proportions. He is now working "behind the scenes" facili-
tating the professionalization of road running.

But Jack Bacheler, now a professor of entomology and an
award winning distance coach at North Carolina State, will
always remember Galloway for a very different reason. In the
1972 Olympic trials, Shorter and Galloway easily made the

team by finishing 1-2 in the 10,000, but number three muske-
teer Bacheler managed to get disqualified for getting into a
shoving match with Jon Anderson in the final stretch as they
sprinted for the last spot.

"I'll never forget what Jeff did in the marathon trials later,"
he said. "Frank won it, and Ken Moore was second, but Jeff ran
every step of the way right beside me. He did it for the specific
purpose of getting me on the team. When we came into the
stadium and up to the finish line, he slowed down a little and
let me finish third." There was no question that Galloway
would have preferred to run the marathon in Munich, and that
Bacheler would have rather run the 10,000. Their request to
switch events was later turned down by the coaches for reasons
only that rare breed can fathom. Bacheler went on to finish 9th
in the marathon, but Galloway failed to qualify for the 10K
final. A year or so later, Bacheler went to a birthday party held
at the private school owned and run by Galloway's father in
Atlanta.

"There were a lot of testimonials and complimentary stories being told about Jeff that night, but when they introduced
me, I was referred to as the guy who helped Jeff get to Lake
Tahoe to train for the Olympic team. It became very obvious
that he hadn't told anyone about what he had done. I don't
think he has to this day."

These days the old Gladbagger, now 36, can usually be
found at the Phidippides home office in Atlanta, which is surely one of the few corporate headquarters in America that sports
the colorful athletic laundry of its officers hanging from the
railing outside the front door. It is there, in that combination
warehouse/office building/locker room that the visitor encounters Galloway and finds just how remarkably little some things
change: The Ghandiesque head swivels around quickly and
fixes you with those two piercing hazel orbs, locking in on the
particulars of your existence with the perceptive capabilities of
a pair of Gorz-Borjkow bombsights. Such are the eyes of
Galloway when they are upon you, and no matter who you are,

President of the US Olympic Committee, a runner with a case of shin splints, or just the guy come to paint the walls, the unmistakable impression is that you are the most interesting person in the tri-state area.

"Hey boy!" he says gleefully. Those who have made his acquaintance over the years should count themselves lucky that he wasn't selling cemetery plots or liquid soap distributorships.

"Ah, if we could only bottle that. . ." said Phidippides VP Richard Calmes wistfully. What he is talking about is that *sincerity*, and indeed, they *have* tried to bottle it. They have done remarkably well at it. But for Galloway, the success and grow of the stores is treated as a matter of serendipity.

"Started back in '73," he says in his down home way. "Yup, back in '73, just sellin' shoes right out of the trunk of Mobley, muh car. . ." He looks bemused, as if he can't quite figure it all out himself, and would be grateful if someone could offer a reasonable explanation.

Right after the 1972 Olympics, Galloway went back to Tallahassee where he had received his masters in history at Florida State. "We lived in a little place furnished with bean bags and a thick rug," recalls George West, a roommate of that era. "Jeff always ran in the woods west of town, a pretty wild place he called 'Mount Florida.' When a visiting runner would come to town, Jeff would try to psych them out by saying, 'Hey, let's run on over to Mount Florida and kill some rattlesnakes!' "

Galloway found a partner and opened the first Phidippides in Tallahassee, but soon moved to his home town Atlanta where the real action seemed to be. He opened a store in the Ansley Mall that quickly became a runner's landmark, and the irrepressible Galloway became Atlanta's Mr. Running. He was a promoter par excellence, and the results began to show in the Peachtree entries. Less than two hundred used to finish the race in the early 70's; entries were cut off at 25,000.

Business prospered as well, and Galloway began selling

franchises. As befitting an organization that once operated out of the trunk of Mobley, he stressed the personal element, a far cry from the shoe 'em and shed 'em treatment runners felt they received in other stores. And too, there was the undeniable expertise that an Olympic competitor could offer. When he talks of the Phidippides philosophy, the old bombsights get very wide: "It may seem strange to some people, but it really gives me a good feeling when I see someone walking out of the store with exactly the right pair of shoes." There is a hint of that old missionary zeal in his voice, but he doesn't seem to proselytize, even when he talks of offering his franchisees "a whole new way of life."

Yet despite the rapid growth of the chain, trouble soon came to the Land of Waffle Bottoms. Phidippides International lost 10 stores in the past several years, and a few others are still in trouble. "We were a naive group," Galloway says about the early franchising days. "We didn't know anything about business and we didn't think we needed to."

Little attention was paid to such trivia as standardized bookkeeping, inventory procedures, and advertising systems. New owners were furnished with the Phidippides logo, some shoes and shorts, and a good healthy dose of the old sincerity, and told to go get 'em. What is remarkable in retrospect is just how well most of the stores done. Anyone familiar with the small business scene in America could have predicted big trouble.

"One guy's record keeping system consisted of a bunch of sales slips in a box," said Galloway of one defunct store. "That's it. No ledgers, no inventory, just the box."

Such an approach may have been all right in the old days (indeed, his old Tallahassee friends claim Galloway abjured even the box of sales slips in his early merchandising days), but when the competitive storm came to the aerobic marketplace, the weak stores went down like withered elms.

VP Calmes is given much credit for standardizing Phidippides procedures, getting professional help on such critical items as store design and marketing strategies. He is a lanky former architect who whips around Atlanta in a fire engine red sports car, trying to tie up all the loose ends left by the human buzz bomb. He talks of his old friend and boss with a curious mixture of admiration and incredulity.

"He never writes anything down. When he does, he loses the paper." So much for Jeff Galloway, the organizer. Calmes leaves the impression that the more the boss is out of town doing promotions, visiting stores, laying that *sincerity* on folks, the better things go on the home front. "While he was out of town last week, I changed the logo. People couldn't read it, didn't know what it was. So I changed it. Just like that. Owners loved it. Don't tell him, though. He doesn't know about it yet."

The transformation from a slap-dash-down-home enterprise to a hard-nosed business empire came about after some recent soul searching. "We sat down about a year and a half ago and asked ourselves where we were going," said Galloway. "We decided that if we were going to do this thing, we were going to do it right."

"We already had the expertise, the product knowledge," said Calmes, "and we had a merchandizing philosophy that stressed personal attention, caring about the customer. We have now put together the systems to make sure you can't screw up even if you try. We think we have the best package to offer someone who wants to go into the business now."

Now if they can just keep the old Gladbagger out on the road somewhere.

Jeff Galloway lives with wife Barbara (herself almost a 3-hour marathoner) north of Atlanta next to a park honeycombed with running trails. Both are early risers and they spend much of the morning on a long run (they go separate ways), and on those tasks that require quiet contemplation. Galloway confesses to an interest in writing fiction lately, but says he does it primarily for his own satisfaction.

Late in the morning, the Galloways head into town where Jeff divides his time between the Ansley Mall store and the corporate headquarters. Barbara works at the Ansley Mall store, putting her considerable knowledge to work helping customers. They both travel around the country a good bit, visiting stores, going to races and generally spreading the aerobic gospel.

It is a lifestyle many would envy, yet Galloway shows signs of the old restlessness. "I've been thinking a lot about the future lately," he confesses. "Frankly, I can't tell you what I will be doing in five years. I haven't taken anything out of the company, it's all been plowed right back in. To tell the truth, I could walk away from it tomorrow without a dime and it would all have been worthwhile. The people we've met, the experiences. . ."

Not that it's all been a bed of posies. There was litigation over the sale of the Phidippides name by his former Tallahassee partner, recently settled amicably in Galloway's favor. There was some early ill will when Galloway decided to go on his own rather than signing up with Jimmy Carnes' fledgling Athletic Attic group (the embers of that little barbecue smolder to this day). There is even the Atlanta podiatrist with whom there is a continuing difference of opinion over some bunion-related issue or another.

There is even the fact that due to various political machinations and personality differences, the Peachtree Road Race no longer seems to need the services of either Phidippides or the human buzz bomb.

What to others would be wounds of a most personal nature are to Galloway mere trifles, gnats in the lemonade of life. Such an outlook has brought him a long way from the days when he played second fiddle on the 1966 Wesleyan University cross country team to a fellow named Amby Burfoot. Neither of them felt particularly intimidated by a freshman teammate who would also make good. Burfoot went on to become a writer and a kind of guru for the ultra-distance set, Galloway went on to become an Olympian and businessman, and the freshman went on to become Bill Rodgers.

When Rodgers was herded into Atlanta recently along with a gaggle of Public Relations folks for a Diet Pepsi 10K, his most pressing concern was ducking out of the tapings, interviews and flesh-pressings long enough to go arrowhead hunting with his old buddy Galloway.

It says something about the nature of the sport these days that Rodgers was in town two days before the pair even had a chance to say hello, and that was on the starting line of the race. (Results: Rodgers 1st in 29:14, Gladbagger somewhere back in a respectable 31:36.)

"I remember one of the first races we ran together," said Rodgers. "It was a five miler and I was running along thinking how well I was doing when Jeff just came flying by. . ."

Rodgers maintains an aura, even when engulfed in waves of autograph seekers, of a man who got on the wrong subway. He's not particularly upset about taking the ride, but he's really not sure where the whole thing is headed.

"I remember Sid Sink—you know, the Bowling Green runner who held the American steeplechase record for while—I remember him saying once: 'You know what I'd really like to do in life? I'd like to be a professional runner.' I thought to myself, this guy is crazy.' " So much for Bill Rodgers, the prophet.

Galloway would say that the aerobic movement was inevitable in this land of paper-pushers and video terminal jockeys, and that its continued success is assured by the same factors. Although he would like to improve upon his 2:16 marathon time, he doesn't think he'll ever attain the shape he enjoyed when he ran a 28:15 for 10K on the track in 1972. Yet that seems to matter very little to him. He seeks only a role to play, a receptacle for his endless flow of energy.

Even as Rodgers is still handing out the trophies and smiling for the Instamatics, Galloway is already into his Saturday morning buzz bomb mode; cruising into town and zeroing in on the Ansley Mall store. Hark! Here is a project worthy of the old Gladbagger. The new sign is there, a giant thing, big as a carpet, ready to be mounted up over the store entrance. Just one thing; it needs the mounting holes drilled in it and nothing would do but for the president and chairman of the board of Phidippides International to grab a Black and Decker variable-speed drill and commence punching those holes himself.

Why, in the old days in Tallahassee, he was said to have gotten along on $10 a week ("I think he grazed in the back yard," said one old hand from those days) so no one's going to go out looking for any time-and-a-half, $12.75 an hour carpenter on Saturday morning. It's not penury, It's a matter of, well, why waste money on such things when the human buzz bomb needs nothing so much as a new project?

May, 1981

Second edition note: Jeff Galloway continues to thrive, though the Phiddipides chain has become a victim of the mass merchandisers. Most are gone now, but the original store is still there at Ansley Mall, and there are still rangy-looking real runners helping people try on shoes. Galloway is, of course, widely known through his books, lectures and camps.

September, 1988

Guard Yours

Abook so good, people will steal 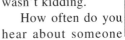 it. That's what one reviewer said. And he wasn't kidding.

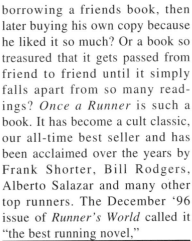

How often do you hear about someone borrowing a friends book, then later buying his own copy because he liked it so much? Or a book so treasured that it gets passed from friend to friend until it simply falls apart from so many readings? *Once a Runner* is such a book. It has become a cult classic, our all-time best seller and has been acclaimed over the years by Frank Shorter, Bill Rodgers, Alberto Salazar and many other top runners. The December '96 issue of *Runner's World* called it "the best running novel,"

Once a Runner, by John L.Parker ©1978, 194 pgs. **$12.95**

The Long Road

You'll find your heart racing right along with the protagonist in this compelling story, beautifully told by a veteran runner. The grand

daddy of all marathons is the backdrop, with the chapters taking you right through the great race itself: Brookline to Hopkinton, Hayden Rowe Street, Ashland, etc.

Long Road to Boston by Bruce Tuckman ©1988, 169 pgs. **$12.95**

A Great One

This critically acclaimed novel, first published in 1969, has for years been regarded as one of the true classics not only in the literature of foot racing, but in general interest literature as well.

There are echoes of *Loneliness of the Long Distance Runner* as well in this story of the working-class stiff, Ike Low, as coach Sam Dee "discovers" him thrashing through inconsequential races, a mediocre sprinter at a local running club.

The Olympian by Brian Glanville ©1969, 253 pgs. **$12.95** Code: **OLY**

Moore's Finest

This book is a continuing source of joy. Moore brilliantly captures some of the most fascinating runners from a particularly interesting era (the

late 70's-early 80's) in distance running and this book offers some of the best non-fiction writing ever done on the subject of running.

Best Efforts by Kenny Moore ©1982, 1992, 199 pgs. **$12.95**

Alleged Humor

Parker's humor collection contains "Flo Jo's Folly," "Life Among Skinflints," and classic Parker commentary on runners' gadgets, traveling in Greece, and "Why I Hate Cross Country."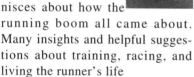

Run Down Fired Up & Teed Off
by John L. Parker, Jr.
©1993, 80 pgs. **$6.95**

The Revolution

Long-time *Runner's World* editor and one of the true veteran commentators of our sport, Joe Henderson, reminisces about how the running boom all came about. Many insights and helpful suggestions about training, racing, and living the runner's life

The Running Revolution
by Joe Henderson
©1980, 205 pgs. **$6.95**

The Great Corbitt

The hard-to-find biography of the legendary 1950's ultra pioneer, Ted Corbitt, a black athlete in a sport that was all but invisible at the time. Also filled with hard-earned training wisdom. Very inspirational.

Corbitt by John Chodes
©1974 154 pgs. **$12.95**

The Vulture Lurks!

The best writers in the sport of running take up a fascinating subject, the last frontier of long-distance events: races longer than a marathon. Who runs these 50-milers, 100-milers, multi-day events, multi-event events? And *why* do they do it?

"Each story is different; each is good enough to stand alone; together each contributes to an outstanding volume."—David Meyers, *Running Journal*

And Then the Vulture Eats You
Ed. by John L. Parker, Jr
©1990, 166 pgs. **$12.95**

Always Young

Every year at the Boston Marathon, the crowds linger long after the leaders have gone by. They wait to cheer another Boston champion, a champion for all seasons and for all  times: the nearly immortal Johnny Kelly. He finished his first Boston in 1933 at age 25, won his first in 1935 at age 27, and has run it every year except one since his first, completing the event 61 times, including 1992.

Young at Heart by Fred Lewis,
©1992, hard, 208 pgs. **$16.95**

Sheehan Retro

The moving, inspiring tribute to George Sheehan, the famed running writer, beautifully assembled by his friend, Joe Henderson, with essays and remembrances from many of Sheehan's friends, relatives and fans from over the years. A must for every serious reader/runner's library.

Did I Win? Ed. by Joe Henderson ©1995 190 pgs. **$12.95**

DeMar Legend

The superb autobiography of the legendary 7-time Boston winner who won in 1937 at age 42, a runner truly ahead of his time. He was a shrewd analyst, yet cautiously open to new ideas. Nearly all the conclusions DeMar reached about training and nutrition 50 years ago have been validated by later research.

Marathon by Clarence DeMar ©1937, 156 pgs. **$12.95**

Incredible Journey

The story of 73-year-old Paul Reese's run across the entire United States, a marathon a day for 124 days straight, covering 3,192 miles.

"The book shows that I am not blessed with super genes," Reese writes, "I've been bothered by a bad back, and I've been treated for prostate cancer. The lesson here is that in life you dance the best you can with the music being played."

Ten Million Steps by Paul Reese ©1994, 226 pgs. **$12.95**

Smart Training

Roy Benson is the highly regarded Atlanta coach /physiologist who has helped pioneer the "effort-based training" concept. Here he provides an easy-to-understand, systematic approach to training using the latest physiological findings. A heart monitor is helpful (since it is an excellent indication of effort) but since Benson is able to scientifically relate all levels of conditioning and ability to pace, the monitor is not strictly required.

The Runner's Coach by Roy Benson, ©1994, 128 pgs. **$12.95**

For Women Only

The personal background, best marks, annual progression, and weekly training schedules of some of the best runners in the country.

How Women Runners Train ©1980, 128 pgs. **$7.95**

ORDER FORM

Quantity	Title	Amount

1. **SUB-TOTAL**	$
2. Florida and Ohio residents please add 7% sales tax	
3. Standard Shipping: Add $3 for 1st book, .50 for each additional	
4. Special Shipping (optional): See box at left, write choice here:	
5. **TOTAL ENCLOSED**	$

Name_____

Address_____

City_____State_____Zip_____

Country_____

Dayphone_____Night phone_____

Important: please furnish phone numbers in case we need to contact you.

☐ Check or money order enclosed (do not send cash)

☐ Visa/Mastercard

Card No._____Expiration____/____

Signature_____

Telephone: 800-548-2388
Fax Orders: 513-849-1624
E-mail: Balbert@AOL.COM

TO ORDER BY MAIL

Send check, money order, or credit card authorization above to:
Cedarwinds Publishing Company
P.O. Box 351 -- 1305 Park Dr.
Medway, OH 45341